Kids Don't Get Cancer

The Remarkably Inspiring Story of Michael Crossland

By Michael Crossland

INTERNATIONAL #1 BESTSELLER

#1 International Amazon Best Seller in 6 Countries

Copyright

By MICHAEL CROSSLAND

First Published 2016 for Michael Crossland by Evolve Global Publishing

PO Box 327 Stanhope Gardens NSW 2768

info@evolveglobalpublishing.com

www.evolveglobalpublishing.com

Book Layout: © 2016 Evolve Global Publishing

www.evolveglobalpublishing.com.au

ISBN: (Paperback) 978-1944788773

ISBN: (Hardcover) 978-1945176791

ISBN-13: (Createspace) 978-1523759712

ISBN-10: (Createspace) 1523759712

ISBN: (Smashwords) 9781310453991

ASIN: (Amazon Kindle) B018J9VJYE

This book is available on Barnes & Noble, Kobo, Apple iBooks (digital), Google Books (digital)

Corporate Speaking Engagements:

Michael has been speaking and working in the corporate sector for over 10 years.

He possesses a powerful ability to tailor his messages to the challenges of the corporate world, and he routinely provides his audience with concrete and intuitively-appealing ideas and principles to assist others to improve their own personal and professional lives.

Michael is regularly asked to provide keynote presentations, and in addition, he's also regularly invited to share his prodigious skills in delivering customer service and sales health checks in the following contexts:

- 1 on 1 sessions
- Team building activities
- Customer service reviews
- Sales training and development
- Sales and service audits
- Customer perception checks

Inquire at www.michaelcrossland.com to book Michael for your next corporate event today.

GET KIDS DON'T GET CANCER
On Audiobooks

Available from:

Or Visit www.michaelcrossland.com MICHAEL CROSSLAND

CONTENTS

Dedication 9

Testimonials 11

Foreword 15

About The Author 17

Introduction..19

Chapter One: Before I Was Born.......................................25

Chapter Two: Such An Innocent Day

That Changed Our Lives Forever 29

Chapter Three: Treatment 35

Chapter Four: Phone Call Of Hope 47

Chapter Five: Dreams Save Lives...................................55

Chapter Six: The Day That Was Never To Happen....................59

Chapter Seven: Heart Stopped At Age 12!!!!...................65

Chapter Eight: Blood, Sweat And Tears.........................73

Chapter Nine: So Began My Career Or Was It 89

Chapter Ten: Living Into My Legacy............................ 101

Chapter Eleven: Power Of Giving....................................113

Chapter Twelve: Tools To Shift Your Mindset....................129

Chapter Thirteen: Where To From Here?.............................141

Chapter Fourteen: Connecting With Michael............................145

**Too often in life, people use their adversities as the reasons
why they fail, instead of using their adversities
as their motivation to succeed.**

In Australian culture, heroes are often portrayed as sports people or millionaires. They might be a cricket player scoring a double century, a footballer scoring a hat-trick of several tries in one match, or an IT technician developing a new generation of smart phones, but the real heroes are those normal, every day people who are faced with extreme challenges and adversity, but who never give up. They fight, they stand strong, and they come out on the other side with a smile on their face and a story to tell.

Michael Crossland is a prime example of a true hero. Michael faces extreme challenges every day of his life, but he stands tall and ensures that his courage and his positive outlook on life inspire other people across the world.

DEDICATION

This book is dedicated to a lady who sacrificed so much in her life, a lady who walked away from her husband and three daughters for numerous years in order to instil love, optimism, courage and hope into a young life that was supposed to end far too soon.

I dedicate this emotional recount of my life to my amazing mum, Kerri.

She inspired me to always work hard, to try my best and to never quit, regardless of what others may say!

Mum, you will forever be my mother, and you will forever remain the heart and soul of our family.

You have always taught us to shoot for the moon, and you constantly reminded us that even when we miss, we will still end up in the stars.

I am forever grateful for your belief that miracles do happen. I love you dearly, and even when the doctors said it was hopeless and to take me home to die, you never walked away. You have filled my soul with hope forever.

TESTIMONIALS

"Michael Crossland was truly one out of the box. His story was, at times, heart wrenching, but the overarching message of refusing to let adversity define you struck a chord with our audience that I don't believe we have hit before, or will manage to again. Never have I seen 500 people leap to their feet so quickly in a unified standing ovation. As a professional speaker, Michael's attention to detail, ability to speak to brief and skill with an audience's focus, was second to none. From a booking point of view, he was friendly, approachable and entirely focused on what we were trying to achieve at our event. I cannot recommend him enough."

Stephanie Wells – Marketing Communications Manager
Franchise Council Australia

"Words escape me to truly express my thanks for the amazing journey you took us all on today as the keynote speaker at the HR Teams event in Sydney and the roller coast ride of emotions you evoked in us all. I feel incredibly humbled and honoured to have met you and want you to know how much you touched everyone in the room today (myself included) with your warmth, passion, incredible spirit and courage in the face of such adversity.

The room was charged full of raw energy and emotion when you finished and many members commented to me afterwards how incredibly inspirational you were and how powerful your messages, learnings and insights were. My congratulations.

I feel very privileged to have met you and wish you well on your continued inspirational journey."

Amanda McKernan | Director
International HR Director Forum | CEO Forum Group

"Thank you for sharing your inspiring, yet very personal, story at our company Kick Start event earlier this year.

From business to sport you reminded us that in life anything we set our mind to we can accomplish successfully. You are a true inspiration to us all."

John McGrath – Chief Executive Officer – McGrath Estate Agents

Michael

"I wanted to drop you both a short note to convey our thanks for a great presentation last Friday morning. Our staff and players thoroughly enjoyed the opportunity to hear your story and were genuinely inspired by your powerful life experiences.

Look forward to catching up with you soon & thanks again for making the time & effort last week."

Todd Greenberg - Chief Executive Officer - BULLDOGS RUGBY LEAGUE CLUB

"Thank you for joining us in Melbourne to share your incredible story with the team at Buxton. Your achievements in the face of adversity in both business and sport are truly remarkable. Hearing about your tenacity and persistence in the face of so many hurdles was inspirational and highly motivating for those of us who work in a competitive sales environment and have our wins and disappointments, albeit no comparison with yours. Perhaps your experience in sales and sales management helped but we felt you connected particularly well with our people from the outset and the feedback since has been nothing short of exceptional. We are all better for the experience. "

Gavan Fallon - Managing Director - Buxton Real Estate Group Pty Ltd

"The feedback from our Leadership was fantastic and after assessing the feedback sheets 100% of the delegates rated your session as Excellent! It was wonderful to have you share your story with our team again."

Olivia Walsh | Organisational Learning & Development Manager CBRE

FOREWORD

During my fifteen years as the CEO of Camp Quality, I have had the great pleasure and privilege of getting to know Michael. After facing extreme emotion and distress, Michael has become a true embodiment of resilience and hope. His relationship with Camp Quality spans over 30 years, following a diagnosis just shy of his first birthday. Now an ambassador and volunteer for the children's cancer charity, Michael is helping to bring the best quality of life to kids and their families who are living with cancer across Australia.

Michael is one of the most inspirational people I have ever met. A man full of humility and gratitude, his passion for life is immeasurable and I've come to see that his biggest determination is to simply give back to the world.

In his autobiography, "Kids Don't Get Cancer", Michael cleverly depicts the tales of his inconceivable life in a style that's graceful, heart-jolting and, at times, ridiculously funny. From early life right through to his time today, it's a page-turning read that will leave you feeling completely in awe of his journey.

Michael's story is one of courage and relentless optimism triumphing over adversity, a message we regularly communicate to our registered kids and families who are on one of life's most testing journeys. Michael is living proof that with an optimistic attitude, you can conquer even the greatest of feats and I'm proud and honoured to have this remarkable young man in our Camp Quality family.

Simon Rountree
CEO – Camp Quality. www.campquality.org.au

ABOUT THE AUTHOR

As one of Australia's most sought -after inspirational speakers, Michael has defied the odds of a life-threatening cancer to build his life of exceptional achievements.

He is a regular inspirational speaker for corporations, schools, professional sporting organisations and universities throughout the world. Michael has presented in front of over 250,000 people around the globe.

His journey has been shared on many TV programs, including Fox Sports, ABC, Channel Seven and Nine networks, Full Potential TV, The Get Inspired Project, Inspire Me Today program and countless radio shows throughout America, Fiji and Australia.

Along with his award-winning program about his life on Australian Stories, Michael has also recently featured in a humanitarian documentary about the countless lives saved through his orphanage and school in Haiti with which he is involved.

Diagnosed before his first birthday and spending over a quarter of his life in hospital, doctors told him school and sport were not options. Infection and fatigue were too great a risk, and reaching his teenage years would be a miracle.

His only wish was to lead a normal life and be able to do all the things that other kids took for granted every day.

But he had a dream and an undying determination to achieve the impossible, irrespective of the size of the obstacles that lay ahead.

Now, an accomplished businessman, National Ambassador for Camp Quality, Australian of the Year finalist, Australia Day Ambassador for numerous consecutive years and International Hall of Fame inductee, Michael inspires people from all walks of life.

There is no doubt he has a heart for giving and a skill to engage people from all walks of life.

He has gone from being one of the youngest State Development Managers for one of the largest companies in the world, to running five banks. He then left his finance career to follow his dreams in making a global impact, and he has certainly done that!

Michael's story "Field of Dreams" was documented on Australian Story, ABC television. Through this documentary, his message touched the hearts of a nation; it's the story of how he overcame seemingly insurmountable obstacles to achieve success in both his personal and professional life.

INTRODUCTION

I am very blessed and privileged to live a wonderful life. I've had the chance to speak to the troops in Iraq who are fighting for our freedom. I have spent time with children in juvenile detention centres throughout America; a large proportion of these young kids, aged between 11 and 15, made just one bad choice and one bad decision, and as a result, their freedoms and liberties were irrevocably withdrawn. These kids with whom I recently met in Texas were all incarcerated due to molestation charges. It is almost impossible to comprehend the adversity that they have experienced for them to be branded criminals as mere children.

It begets the question: What type of environment were they raised in for them to consider their behaviour acceptable in any way, shape or form?

I have had the opportunity to spend time with the victims and families of the September 11 attacks of 2001. These people had their lives completely destroyed by an attack that was as abhorrent as it was unforeseen.

Yet, they still manage to get out of bed every single day of their lives, and they work hard to smile. Regardless of the pain, the suffering and the challenges that they continue to face, they still somehow manage to push through.

I was speaking to a gentleman about his experience as a victim of the September 11 attacks. He was working in one of the buildings on the 25th floor when it happened. He recalls being told to stay in his cubicle, to stay calm, and not to move.

He went on to say: "There was something telling me to get out, take the stairs and run". He ran down 25 flights of stairs, and whilst in the stairwell, he heard a massive explosion and assumed that the building was about to crush him. Nevertheless, he kept running.

When he finally reached the ground floor, he ran outside, only to find what looked like a war zone. He looked over and saw that the explosion he heard earlier was the second tower, which had also been hit. He ran from the building and could hear loud, slapping noises.

He got far enough away, turned, and to his horror, he saw that the slapping noise was people hitting the pavement whilst trying to escape the burning building.

These stories are reminders to people that life is a gift; we need to embrace it and enjoy it whilst we can. Our lives can be turned upside down with just one phone call, one bad decision, one act of terror, and our lives may never be the same again.

I am a strong believer that it's not about the amount of years you live on this earth. Instead, what you fit into those years towards helping to make the world a better place is what really matters.

There's a great proverb: "I cried when I didn't get a new pair of shoes, until I saw a boy who had no feet." I think it's very important that we develop a habit of stepping out of our own shoes to look at life through someone else's eyes.

This practice allows us to realise how lucky we are to have what we have. I think it's so important that we count our blessings instead of our problems.

Over the last few years, I have been presented with numerous opportunities to address large audiences as a speaker across different world locations. There was one time that has truly changed my life forever. I was on a three-month speaking tour.

I married my high school sweetheart on April 21st and, on the 1st of May, I left the country for three months. I was going to travel around Australia for two months as a speaker, and then I was planning to go to America for a month. In those three months, I had scheduled just two days off, and in those two days, I had planned to head back to Coffs Harbour to spend some time with my lovely wife.

A little while back, I received a phone call from a lady in Adelaide. Her name was Michelle. She said to me: "Michael, I heard you speak a couple of years ago. You really touched me. There's a young boy here in Adelaide. His name is Kai. He's been diagnosed with cancer.

We were wondering whether you could possibly donate your time, come out to Adelaide, and present and raise some money for the family because they're really struggling."

I said: "I'm pretty well booked out until September, but I'll come out when I return and I'll see how much money we can raise for this family." It was all set. I was heading out there. Then, two weeks later, I received a phone call from a lady named Kylie who was also from Adelaide.

Kylie said to me: "Michael, there's a young boy in Adelaide. His name is Kai. He's been diagnosed with cancer." I said: "Yeah, I'm aware of him. I'm heading out there in September".

She replied: "Michael, Kai has just been transferred from the Oncology Ward to the Palliative Care Unit. This little 5- year-old boy has less than two weeks to live, and his one last dying wish is to meet you."

I am no superstar, no professional athlete, and nor am I a famous actor or hero. I stand here today as a man who has faced my fair share of adversity. Regardless, I continue to remember what Mum always told me.

Irrespective of how many times you get knocked down, you just have to keep getting back up. I called my wife and I told her about this. She said, "Those two days you were going to spend with me: I want you to spend them with this little boy."

I remember being on the plane flying to Adelaide from Sydney, and I said to myself: "Don't emotionally connect with this little boy." When I arrived in Adelaide, I got in a car and drove to the hospital. As I walked into the room, a little five-year-old boy ran across the floor and jumped into my arms. Instantly, I was emotionally connected with this little angel.

The little boy, his family and I all went out for a beautiful lunch, played catch, I gave him a few little gifts, and I let him steer the car back through the vineyards. He thanked me for a great day, and he told me that he would see me soon. I could not bring myself to say anything back, because I knew that I would never see that sweet little boy again.

That night, we raised thousands of dollars for the family, and the community's support was overwhelming. Sadly, little Kai was finished fighting, and three weeks later whilst I was in the USA, I received a text message from his Mum. The text read: "My boy is cancer free and pain free". My heart sank and tears flowed down my face unchecked, because of a heroic little boy who lost his battle with cancer.

Most of the money that had been raised to help Kai's family was used to bury beautiful Kai. The tears that continued to well in my eyes for many days after Kai passed away were not just of sadness, but they were also tears of joy in the knowledge that I had experienced the tremendous blessing of spending special moments with Kai.

He was now an angel shinning brightly, and for such a little soul, he had touched the lives of so many.

In his little casket, he was wearing my wristband that I gave him. I know that, regardless of the challenges that I have faced and continue to face, there's been a little boy in this world to whom I have made a difference.

I think that making a difference to others is what life is all about. Life is about waking up every single day, knowing in our hearts that we can make a difference in someone else's life.

Every day, we are in a position to help people to live their dreams, to shape their futures, and above all else, give of ourselves, without expecting anything in return.

CHAPTER ONE

BEFORE I WAS BORN

Time and health are two precious assets that we neither recognise nor appreciate until they have been depleted. Embrace yours now and love every moment.

It was 1983. My mother, Kerri, went to the doctor because there were to be no more kids; my parents had decided that three crazy daughters were enough. The plan was to have her tubes tied. When she got in there, the doctor said:

"Either congratulations or commiserations."

Mum thought maybe there was a problem with her gynaecological health, but when he said he could probably help her out in six months, she knew she was pregnant. Mum was terrified by the prospect of another child, but Dad always wanted a boy.

In fact, he had already named the first, second, and third child Michael, but as he apparently used to say, he missed having a boy each time by half an inch.

My family lived in the beautiful country town of Crossmaglen, which is fifteen minutes south west of Coffs Harbour on the east coast of Australia. We lived on a five acre property with fruit trees, chickens, dogs, a massive vegetable garden, and a few sheep. It was a very tightly-knit community where everyone knew everyone. People were accustomed to helping each other.

Neighbours routinely swapped food and other goods. My Mum called it God's Country. We had properties all around us, most of which were banana plantations . We had a family living behind us who grew ten acres of bananas. My Mum told me that due to a lack of rain at the time, our neighbours sprayed their bananas to get them ready to be sold. Mum discovered much later that before our neighbour made the aerial spray, he had asked his wife to leave the house, because it was suspected that she was pregnant.

At this stage, Mum was seven months pregnant, and the very next day after the bananas were sprayed, she went into an early labour. Fortunately, the medical staff were able to stop the premature labour, and Mum went on to have a full- term pregnancy. To this day, we believe that it was the spray that caused her to go into labour, and we also suspect that it was the cause of many other health challenges.

On the 2nd of May, 1984, Mum had a painless delivery. She said that she was certainly aware that she was in labour with the girls, but she had no idea that she was in labour with me.

During the delivery, a physician by the name of Doctor Scott was our gynaecologist. He waited for Mum to experience signs of labour pain, which never arrived, although she was trying to push.

She started to push, and he noticed that the umbilical cord was wrapped around my throat. He asked Mum to stop pushing, and any woman who has ever given birth will understand that's almost impossible to do at that stage in labour. What Doctor Scott and Dad experienced was something they both described as a miracle.

I turned myself around 360 degrees, freed the cord from around my neck, and out I came. As Doctor Scott held me up in the air, he said: "This child is here for a reason."

My family and extended family were so delighted to add another member to the Crossland household. Dad finally had his son and Mum finally did what needed to be done to ensure there were no more surprises—four children were more than enough.

Life on the farm was ideal—so green, so fresh, and so quiet.

We had a beautiful little fresh water creek that gently flowed through the back part of the property, and we would always swim there and play as a family.

As I reflect on those days, the memories bring me joy, but my reminisces are mixed with some sadness, because as we grow older, we tend to forget about the wonderful moments we shared together as a family, and instead, reflect only on the challenging times. As adults, I think many of us forget to have a good time and to simply enjoy life.

Instead, we get stuck in a rut of trying to be mature and grown-up, until the rare times that we take a moment to look back. It is then that we realise that we are now much older. We have missed much of the excitement of what life is all about.

The good times on the farm with my family were about to come to an end as a dark cloud of fear, heartache and pain was about to take over and consume us all for many long years.

CHAPTER TWO

SUCH AN INNOCENT DAY THAT CHANGED OUR LIVES FOREVER

**The strongest people aren't always the people who win,
but the people who don't give up when they lose.**

I was perfectly healthy, and by all accounts, I was considered a "normal" baby; I ate plenty of food, and I was an active and happy little boy. Mum took me to the baby clinic regularly.

At the age of six months, the medical staff noticed that the growth of my stomach was a little too rapid for my age, but it was not discussed any further at that stage. Mum commented years later that the clinic nurses had simply said that maybe I was just over-indulging, because Mum was still feeding me as well as giving me solid foods.

There were no other symptoms, problems, or sickness, so they just didn't give it another thought. Months later, Mum took me to the doctor with my sister, because my sister had an ear infection. It was that day that our lives were turned upside down, and our entire lives changed forever. My sister Renee was born premature. Consequently, she suffered from a lot of ear, nose, and throat problems in her earlier years. So, my parents took Renee to see our doctor quite regularly, and we were there for another checkup on her ears.

While I was there, Doctor Scott made the comment that he was finally seeing me, because even though he delivered me, he hadn't seen me for ten months. I was a happy, healthy baby, and had not been sick to warrant a

29 | KIDS DON'T GET CANCER

visit. Whilst at the surgery, Mum allowed me to crawl around the floor of the consultation room, and when the doctor picked me up to give me a hug, he noticed the size of my stomach. He made a comment about it, and in reply, Mum explained to him what the health clinic had said.

After he finished examining Renee, Doctor Scott said he wanted to have a look at my stomach. He wanted to feel it to see whether there was anything there. Mum insisted that we needed to go home, because she had a routine with the three girls and me. It was 5:30 in the afternoon. After he felt my stomach, he arranged an immediate ultrasound.

So, we went for an ultrasound at a quarter to six that night. After several doctors looked at the results, they told Mum that Doctor Scott was waiting in his surgery for us to return. That's when it began. Mum said: "There's no way possible that Doctor Scott would still be there at 6:30, because he would have gone home. We have to go home." He was there waiting.

He didn't give us any information about what it was, although he said to Mum that it could possibly be a large build-up of fatty tissue in my stomach. He also said we had to be in Sydney the following day. I guess that was the exact moment when our lives and the lives of everyone else who was a part of our family's lives, changed forever.

After all, it was just the six of us who lived out on the farm at Crossmaglen. Then, without warning, Mum and I were ripped away from the family for many years to come. Mum and I arrived in Sydney, with everyone praying that it was a benign lump in my stomach.

Then Doctor Mary arrived into our lives, and at that stage, the family had no idea she would be a part of it for so many years. She asked Mum whether she knew anything at all about childhood cancer.

Mum's first words were apparently: "Kids don't get cancer". Mum and many of our family members and friends honestly believed that cancer was something you got when you got old.

Doctor Mary then broke the news to Mum: There was a likely probability that I had cancer. Nevertheless, there were a lot more tests and scans that had to be done before the diagnosis could be confirmed. Mum said that her immediate thought was: "It's not true; it just can't be, because kids don't get cancer." Late that afternoon, the diagnosis was confirmed.

To this day, Mum says that it was like time stood still, and the words came out in slow motion. Pain filled my Mum's heart when she heard: "We have found a mass in his stomach; your son has Neuroblastoma Stage 4 of the central nervous system. It is the size of a football, and there are several more throughout his abdominal area.

There's just too much. I am sorry, Kerri his survival rate would be no more than 4%, we can't help him." What do you do when told that it's all over? You can roll over and die, or you can fight to the very end. "There's nothing we can do", they said. In a nutshell, this meant: " Go home with a 96% chance of death." But, in life its not your adversity that defines you; it's how you deal with it.

As you may have already gathered, one of my favourite proverbs is: "I cried when I didn't get a new pair of shoes until I saw a boy who had no feet." To me, this is a tremendously powerful way of saying that we need to compare our challenges and adversities with those of others for us to realise how lucky we truly are.

As a baby, my life was 96% hopeless, but there was still 4% hope, and come hell or high water; my Mum was going to see to it that we never quit. We would be among the 4% who survived.

It was not until we were taken downstairs to the Oncology Ward that reality hit. Years later, Mum commented that when we walked in there, it was the darkest place Mum had ever entered. Inside the ward, there were kids everywhere with no hair, needles up their noses, and parents who were completely heartbroken.

With the help of the hospital staff, we found our room and settled in for what was going to be a very long road. Mum felt so alone; she was so isolated, lost and truly scared of what each day was going to bring. We just needed some hope. Hope is one of the most powerful words in the dictionary, and if we could just get a little taste of hope, then that might be all that was needed to fight a good fight in order to win. My family and friends prayed all day every single day, hoping for a miracle.

More than anything else, my parents hoped that the doctors would actually treat me. Instead, they did more and more tests and continued to say: "We are sorry, but there is just no treatment that would save your son." We couldn't just go home. Mum repeatedly asked whether there was any possibility that the doctors could treat me.

"Surely, there's got to be something!" They relentlessly replied: "No." This went on for four days, however for mum this would have felt like a lifetime. The phone calls to the family back home were heart-breaking. Dad did not know whether to tell my sisters and the rest of the family that I was dying, or to continue to hope and pray.

Today, I try to put myself in my parents' shoes and to imagine how they dealt with this type of fear and pain. I have come to the conclusion that you can simply never understand until you walk in the same shoes. I pray that I never walk in those shoes.

Doctor Mary came in to see me and my Mum on the fifth day of my hospitalisation. She said they had two American doctors visiting the hospital. She was going to put my case to them. "Still there is no hope, so don't get carried away."

So, my Mum waited and waited with me for three hours, which she has said many times since, felt more like three weeks. Mum's heart was racing and tears flowed freely down her face, but she said she constantly tried to hide it from me as she didn't want me to see that she was upset. Then, slowly the door opened.

Doctor Mary came through the door with an emotionally detached look on her face: "Kerri, they're prepared to have a look and try, but they promise nothing." Mum cried out loud, as if they had found a cure purely because our hearts finally had a little hope in them. Mum hugged me so tight and didn't want to let me go.

I think there's plenty of times in people's lives where they're faced with a challenge where they just want to quit. They just want to walk away. They think it's too hard. It goes without saying that I'm so grateful every day that Mum didn't quit on me. Mum's outlook on life, her courage and optimism has, no doubt, continued to shape me and many others throughout my journey.

Obviously, there was still a lot of fear and worry for my family, because I was so sick. Mum believes, as a parent, you would do everything and give your utmost for your children, whether it is treating them for a common cold or a broken arm. She believes that any parent would stand by their child no matter how dire the situation, and do everything in their power to get their children through their battles.

It was a massive sacrifice for Mum to be away from my three sisters and our Dad for such long periods of time in hope that the treatment worked.

We were a seven hour drive from our home town, and with very minimal money, there was no way that we could afford regular visits or even trips home when my white cell count was up.

CHAPTER THREE

TREATMENT

**"Every day holds the possibility of a miracle. Keep striving;
it might be behind the very next door."** Michael Crossland

When the doctors suggested they'd start the treatment, Mum said they provided her with a summary of what the treatment would involve. Again, there were more tears and mounting fears within the family. Mum poorly understood the chemotherapy and doctor speech, but years later, she said she was just happy they were going to try to save me. The doctors came in to inform Mum that they were going to start me on my treatment.

The first round was going to start on the 2nd of May. The medical staff apparently kept reminding Mum that the odds of my survival were extremely low. The family didn't really take that news into consideration. Instead, they merely thought: "Treatments are starting, so we've got hope." One of the doctors said: "They'll be starting in the morning", which coincided with the very first anniversary of my birth—I was barely a year old. Mum remembers asking the medical staff whether we could hold off for just one day so that I could enjoy my special day with my family, but their reply was as definite as it was immediate: "Every minute counts".

Rather than focusing on the grim facts and the excruciating side-effects that the treatments would have on my tiny body, my family later explained to me that they had decided to see the first day of my treatment as marking the time that we started to beat this cruel and insidious disease.

As Mum told me when I was old older, a cake arrived the very next morning, bearing one little candle. Nevertheless, it was a very short-lived celebration; one moment, the candle was blown-out, and the next, one of the doctors marched through the door, followed by some of the nurses. It was time to commence round one of chemotherapy treatment, which provided my best hope of survival. My family really had no idea whatsoever how it was going to make me feel, or the impact that it was going to have on my body.

On the first day of my treatment, the doctor located my strongest vein, and through my strongest vein the first lot of chemotherapy was injected. Years later, Mum told me that her immediate reaction was a feeling of excitement, but her belief that this was the stuff that was going to both rapidly and very effectively make me better, turned out to be very short-lived.

Within five minutes, I started projectile vomiting, and the vomiting could not be stopped. It was as violent as it was persistent. In fact, according to Mum, the vomiting was so intense that the back of my throat became so badly burned it would bleed. Then, after the vomiting stopped, I could not eat, because the burns turned into painful and tender blisters. At the start of my treatment, my cycle was nine days on and three days off, and after every treatment, Mum became more convinced that I was going to die. I was just so sick.

Years later, Mum told me that for a while after the commencement of my treatment, she started to leave the room during the treatment—just so that she could sit outside to get some fresh air. Whilst outside, she would cry so hard, because she was just so helpless; there was just absolutely nothing she could do to either make me better or ease my immense suffering. I recall that as I grew older, my Mum would always try to hide her tears from me, because she would never want me to see her visibly upset.

Regardless of her efforts to hide her sadness from me, I still knew where she was going during my treatments, and I was also intuitively aware of when she was sad. Her eyes were constantly glassy, even though she worked so hard to hide her fear and sadness from me. Her unavailing and selfless strength is something that I will forever admire. To this day, her strength instills me with both inspiration and a determination to be like her.

A number of years after treatment Mum explained she very quickly realised my first round of treatment was not going to equate to a short or temporary hospital visit, because the side effects of the treatment were taking a serious toll on my body. In fact, she recalled one morning she awoke from sleeping in the chair beside my bed, only to see a look of despair, confusion and fear on my face. I was sitting up in bed, holding handfuls of my own hair, and trying to comprehend what was going on.

Throughout the night, my eyelashes and eyebrows had fallen out, and I was starting to look like a gravely ill little boy—much like a number of other children in the ward who had undergone the same treatment and died.

After a year had passed, Mum came to a level of acceptance about where we were headed within the hospital environment, and the journey we had no choice but to take. She was remarkable. She could always see the light and she always managed to maintain her optimism and hope, irrespective of how low and dark our days became during the treatment journey.

Even as a little guy, I apparently always loved to help others. Mum regales stories about what she used to do after I had my chemotherapy. According to Mum, she would try really hard to get me to sleep, because when I went to sleep after chemotherapy, I would not vomit. As time went by, I began to tell the other children in the ward to do exactly the same thing as my Mum kept trying to do for me.

The other children were in their beds, awake, vomiting, and extremely sick and miserable. According to Mum, I would stand up in my cot and instruct the other children:

"Hey, boy; You go to sleep. You won't be sick." This is the sort of thing that I just started to repeat to all of the children, because even though I was too young at the time

to remember it now, it must have worked, and clearly, I was keen to share with the other kids in the ward what had helped me.

On my own, I also worked out that if I counted to one hundred, the needles would be in and the pain in my hand would be gone before I even knew it, so I got very good at counting, and boy, did I learn fast!

After the chemo had really started to kick in, my Mum started carrying me around, like most mothers do! One morning, I just started crying incessantly, and Mum could not understand why. The crying continued for two days, and my Mum said to the doctor: "This is not normal; please do something!"

Doctor Mary ran heaps of tests and found that the drugs had made my bones so brittle that they had cracked. I had several fractures under my armpits, around my elbows and to both knees. This was caused by one of the drugs, called Vin Christine. They stopped the drug immediately and I had to wear a helmet. I was in a cast, and elbow pads and knee pads had to be worn to prevent further damage! It was critical that we protected my bones as the pain was immense.

This went on for two months, and finally, the bones repaired themselves. Unfortunately, Doctor Mary needed to restart the Vin Christine drug again. I can only imagine the pain Mum would have felt being so utterly helpless, and not being able to help or take my pain away.

There were times during the days of chemotherapy treatment that I was not permitted by the medical staff to be outside in the sunlight. Sometimes, there would be around fifteen to twenty kids outside playing baseball, and for once, these kids were actually enjoying their lives. All of the parents had a ball, and we had to run around the yard, still attached to the trolleys that held our intravenous fluids, which in many cases, had become a permanent fixture to our hands.

Doctor Mary would come out to yell at Mum. She'd say: "It's wonderful what you're doing, but Michael's the only child that shouldn't be out there." Mum never wanted to treat me any differently to all of the other kids. For instance, from a young age, she insisted that I use the toilet in the hospital, she taught me how to make my bed, as well as how to use a knife and fork, and ultimately, she made me feel like I was a normal kid—at least I thought so anyway.

Throughout the treatment journey, Mum continued to remain very naive about blood groups, and she also had a poor understanding of the damage that the chemotherapy was doing to my normal bodily functions. On one occasion, I recall it was getting really close to Christmas. Mum just so desperately wanted to go home to be with Dad and the girls so that the family could spend Christmas together.

Regardless, Doctor Mary informed my Mum that my bloods were not good, and that we couldn't go home; we had to stay where we were during the Christmas holidays. I remember that Mum felt so strongly she ended up getting a bit nasty with the doctor, and she accused Doctor Mary of being inhumane.

She even went as far as criticising Doctor Mary for having no consideration for our family. Even as a kid, I felt that Mum's complaints against Doctor Mary were very unfair. Doctor Mary basically acted like an old-school teacher, and she firmly and authoritatively requested for Mum to venture outside my room into the hall, so that she was away from me.

My Mum obediently followed her request, which sounded more like an order, and Doctor Mary followed her into the hall. Even though they were in the hall, I could still hear their conversation.

A s a child, I thought the first question Doctor Mary posed to Mum was really weird: "How old do you think I am?" Years later, Mum said that she had actually tried to be very kind in her answer to the doctor.

She replied, "Strange question, Mary. Around 45?" Mum said she looked much older than that, but she was trying to be really nice, hoping that the Doctor would be flattered by Mum's response and that as a result, she would let us go home to the rest of our family for Christmas.

Doctor Mary sounded weary, although nonchalant about the answer my Mum had given about her age. "I've just turned 39." Doctor Mary had white/grey hair that was pulled back severely into a little pony tail; I suppose it was her hair that made her look older than what she really was, but as a kid, it was hard to tell. I mean, when I was a child, anyone over the age of 15 seemed "old" to me.

She continued to address my Mum: "I just want you to know something... Your 3 daughters? I don't give a damn. Your husband? I honestly don't give a damn about him either. As far as your son is concerned, we are going to do absolutely everything in our power to keep him alive." Mum just sat there, and for once, she had absolutely nothing to say.

I mean, what does a person say after being served an impressive and irrefutable blow like that? Mum just sat there, and years later, she told me that whilst she was sitting there, she repeated the following inside her head, like a mantra: "From now on, it will be: Yes, sir. No, sir. Three bags full, sir." She was extraordinary.

She certainly had the courage to stand-up and fight when others had not wanted to fight for me at all. It was just like Mum; she never quit, and she never let go. Ever.

As time passed in hospital, we came to meet some delightful families, many of whom I still remember. There was one lady in particular who warrants a special mention. Her name was Ingrid. She was Dutch. Her son, Mitchell, had a Wilms' tumor. As it turned out, he had his kidney removed on the first day that I started chemotherapy.

When the very first dose of my chemotherapy started, Mum was absolutely horrified and terrified. It was fairly typical that the medical staff would still be administering the chemotherapy through an IV cannula, when all of a sudden, I would start to projectile vomit. Mum was stricken by what she was seeing.

When I was old enough, Mum told me that one day Ingrid simply just appeared out of nowhere behind her, and she said to her: "Hello; my name is Ingrid." Mum looked up at Ingrid, and Ingrid continued to address my Mum, in front of me and the staff who were administering my treatment: "I know what you're going through. There's not much we can do. How about you and I just go outside?

We will sit down at the tree for five minutes. Then, we will come back, because there's nothing we can do." The nursing staff agreed with Ingrid's suggestion as well as her rationale. In line with Ingrid's suggestion, they said to Mum: "Maybe you really should go outside for a while", because Mum was very distressed by my screaming and by how violently ill the treatment was making me.

So, apparently after slightly more convincing from Ingrid, they retreated outside together to sit under a tree. It was really hard on Mum, but the louder I cried, the louder Ingrid spoke. The more Mum announced: "I've got to go inside", the more Ingrid insisted: "No; you don't. Until they are finished administering the chemotherapy, we will remain sitting outside." From that moment on, Ingrid and Mum became the best of friends, and Ingrid was just a pillar of strength for our entire family. Sometimes in life, we simply need to draw a line down the middle of a page. On the left-hand side, we write down the things that are within our control. On the right-hand side, we write the things that are out of our control. Too often, we spend so much energy focusing on the items that belong on the right-hand side of that page, futilely trying to fix the things that are completely out of our control.

Nonetheless, during the phase of our lives when I was being treated for childhood cancer, more than anything, we really needed to muster all of our energy, our strength, and all of our courage, so that we could begin to focus on the things that were both within our control, and which required our attention. Had we continued to focus on the things over which we had no control whatsoever, neither of us would have coped at all.

Mum rarely left my side. She would be there when I woke each day, and she was always holding my hand when I drifted off to sleep every night.

Due to the volume of tumours I had, the treatment plan was to maintain a shrinkage program for as long as possible; the doctors were going to attempt to shrink my tumours for as long as my body would allow it. One unfortunate attribute of neuroblastoma, which is the type of tumours that I had, is that neuroblastoma has a tendency to build a membrane around itself.

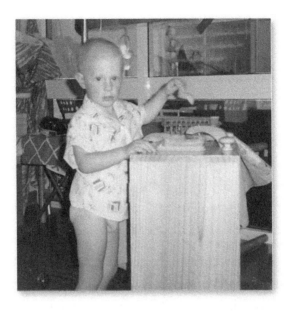

Consequently, it can become resistant to chemotherapy, and most unfortunately, my tumours' resistance to the chemotherapy had slowly become apparent to the medical staff, and more gradually, to my family. This realisation certainly had the impact of raising the fear and distress of my family to unprecedented levels.

There was simply no other choice, the doctors explained: "We have to operate now, because the chemotherapy is not working. Sadly, Kerri, if we don't get it all whilst in surgery, it will be over, and the chances of him coming out of surgery are not great." When they got me prepped for surgery, Doctor Mary came into the room.

They had me on the trolley, all ready to go, and Mary gave an instruction to the wardsman: "Let the Mother carry him." Mum looked at Mary, and Doctor Mary explained: "It could be the last time, Kerri." I can only imagine the overwhelming pain, the terror, and the uncontrolled, raw mixture of emotions that Mum experienced as she carried me into the white room where they were going to cut me open, kissing me for possibly the very last time.

I remember that she was desperately trying to show no emotion at all; it brings tears to my eyes as I type these memories and recall these events. Her devastation and fear had to have been profound, and yet, as always, she kept her emotions in check for my sake.

Prior to my operation, my Mum and Dad had their blood checked to ascertain their blood group. Dad's blood was found to be compatible with mine, so he asked the doctors whether he could possibly donate some of his blood to me. He'd get off the beer. He wouldn't consume anything unhealthy at all, so his blood would be of optimal quality for his son's needs.

The medical staff insisted that it wasn't necessary. Still, Mum and Dad started to become a bit insistent about Dad donating his blood to help me. They wanted to do it, because the HIV virus was poorly understood at that stage, and it was widely believed to be rampant and easily contractible at that time. They wanted to cover all bases. Again, the medical staff insisted to my parents that using Dad's blood to replace my own during the surgery was absolutely unnecessary.

Six hours is the amount of time that the operation took, and Mum waited and waited, constantly praying that all was going to be OK, that her little boy was going to come out alive, and that the doctors would come out of surgery to deliver her the news that she so longed to hear, which was that the surgery had gone like a dream, the tumours had all been removed, there had been no complications, and that ultimately, her little boy would be OK.

Unfortunately, when one of the doctors finally left the theatre to report to my Mum about how the surgery had gone, she did not get what she had prayed for at all. In fact, they said exactly what she feared the most. "Kerri, he is still alive, but only just. We lost him for nearly two minutes, but he is hanging in there.

However, we are sorry, but we didn't get it all, and there is simply nothing more that we can do. Unfortunately, Michael had a very bad bleed through the surgery; he had two bags of blood, which at the time, we weren't concerned about. However, we have been notified that, unfortunately, the blood that we did give him through surgery wasn't screened. Now, we have to undertake five years of AIDS virus screening to ensure that he has not contracted the virus."

Years later, my Mum said that this day was the day she became broken; not only was she a broken Mother, but as of that moment, she had a broken spirit and a lost soul. She could scarcely believe the words that the Doctor had just said, but remarkably, somehow she did not lose hope. She said that the first thing that I said when I came out of surgery was that I wanted an ice block, and that I wanted to play ball.

My family were flown down to Sydney so that they could spend my last few moments with me.

After I came out of surgery, I told my Mum that I went to God's house. Mum tried to convince me that my mind was just playing tricks on me, because of all the flying that I had done, heading back and forth from Sydney to Coffs Harbour. Mum reminded me years later that I told her I was only there for a couple of minutes, sitting on God's lap, looking down on the planes, the hospital, and me in the room.

I said it was so beautiful, that I was so healthy, and so free. God said to me: "Your time is not now, my son. You have a big journey ahead of you". My Mum recalled the surgeon told her I had died on the operating table for nearly two minutes.

She cried in front of me, and she later told me that she felt as though all of her prayers had actually been answered.

The weight, the fear and the worry had been taken from her almost instantaneously, and she felt as though she could breathe again for the first time in a very long time.

I regularly look into the world, and I witness people getting angry and frustrated because of First World problems: There's traffic on the road, or because they are asked to pay six dollars for a bottle of water in a five- star hotel, or it's too hot or too cold.

Every day, every single one of us, regardless of how optimistic or positive we are, complain about trivial, inconsequential, and non life-threatening problems.

It makes me think: "Geez! If only these people were to face real problems and real heartache, would it still be a massive concern for them?" I think that it's so important that we don't wait for the phone call that changes our life, the doctor's visit that fills our hearts with fear, that once in a lifetime decision, or an opportunity that changes everything.

We need to appreciate the finer things in life, love our challenges, grow from the hurdles that we face, and learn every day from every mistakes we make.

CHAPTER FOUR

PHONE CALL OF HOPE

"Faith consists in believing what reason cannot." Voltaire

"When the world says, 'Give up,' hope whispers, 'Try it one more time.'" – Author Unknown

My family was told I was going to be dead within four weeks, but just three days after the doctor had made this announcement, another doctor came into my room. He said to my Mum: "Kerri, we have a test drug. We're going to try it on 25 kids. We've got 24 candidates. We want to give your son the opportunity of a future."

I truly believe that hope is one of the most powerful words in the English dictionary. If you can instill hope in somebody's life, you can instill determination, courage and passion, which can allow you to overcome anything.

I started this test drug at 9:00am on a Tuesday morning. It made all of us kids who were given the drug violently sick; it felt as though my insides were on fire, and none of the kids who were given the treatment were spared of this horrendous side-effect. Within 24 hours, the burning was so severe that we were all transferred from the Oncology Ward to the Burns Unit.

The side effects of this drug were so grievous that we were all covered from head to toe in blisters. The nurses would wrap us up in bandages and lay us in baths full of ice to try to control our temperatures and to prevent our brains from frying. We would just lie there and cry; there was really nothing else we could do. The feeling of being so helpless was unimaginable for all the families who were watching their children go through the most agonising pain.

Within five days, one of the little boys in my room who was also receiving the treatment, tragically passed away. My Mum started to get very scared; she was so terrified of losing me that she could no longer hide her tears. I could see pure, unadulterated fear in her eyes when two more kids passed away from the treatment over the next 48 hours. Within just one month, 20 out of the 25 patients were dead.

I can only imagine what it must be like as a Mother or a Father to be forced to make the decision as to whether to inject the very drug that has killed so many other little children into their own child. Mum said that the hardest part about that journey was watching the tiny body bags that held deceased little children who had died from the same drug I was on, being wheeled out of the very room I had shared with them.

Within the second month of the treatment, the drug began to burn my internal organs, and I had sustained severe burns to my left lung. My liver and my kidney were also being destroyed, while the muscles around my heart began to deteriorate. By the third month of being administered the drug, I was the only one left in the big room that had once been filled with 24 other families. Within 90 days, 24 out of the 25 were dead. My Mum was faced with an impossible decision: She could either decide to continue the treatment, which meant the decision to continue to burn me, with a very real possibility of having the same fate as the other kids who had died, or alternatively, stop the treatment, with the guarantee that I would die.

Constantly seeing the other kids leave the room, one by one, and not return, really escalated Mum's fears. At that stage, she started to direct her thoughts, feelings and communications towards cancer survivors. I think that was what gave her hope; she had to draw on the the strength that these survivors gave her in order to instill true hope in her own heart. The tragedy of witnessing the deaths of so many other children was incredibly hard to deal with. You'd see them one week, and then the following week they'd be gone. There was a little boy who had Stage 2 neuroblastoma.

We had seen him only two weeks prior to the day that he had finally gone home. Mum had tried really hard to connect with and relate to this family, because for far too long, she had only dreamed of one day taking me home.

Then one day, that same little boy was lying on the floor back in the hospital. Mum said to his Mum: "Why are you back? It looks like he has the mumps." Unfortunately, he had suffered a massive relapse. As it turned out, he had over 30 tumors growing out of his body, and two days later, he was dead. That day was the day Mum took herself to St. Mary's Cathedral. She went to a healing service with the intention of casting all of her burdens to the Lord to lighten the load. Mum says her first thoughts were: "This one's too heavy for anyone to carry". Still, she said she managed to hand it all over. She replaced her fear with faith, and years later, she commented that the strength she gained from that experience truly got her through. It was on the day of her visit to St. Mary's Cathedral that she began to realise she was not alone, and the darkest and heaviest days were the days she was being carried.

Every single day, I know in my heart that I've had a much easier life than my Mum. The only thing I had to contend with is the pain. On the other hand, my Mum had to helplessly watch her tiny son in pain, whilst remaining absolutely helpless, and not only that, she had to make impossible decisions about my treatment. I cry every time I think of how it must have been for her. This realisation is what has always prevented me from sitting around and feeling sorry for myself. Instead, it has only spurred me on to keep fighting, to strive for greatness, and to absolutely never give- up.

Life was very hard to take at times. Whilst in isolation, we were allowed no visitors. If Mum came in to see me, she had to wear a gown and a mask. Mum told me in later years that she tried so hard not to cry in front of me. She used to walk outside and sit on the veranda to hide her tears, and I would constantly be calling out for her. I am sure most people agree that life just gets too hard sometimes, and during those times, the only thing we can manage to do is to hope that it gets a little easier. Well, thanks to one very special lady, it did! We got very close to a nurse by the name of Jo Gooch. She was an oncology nurse, who was absolutely amazed by my Mum's courage and by the battles that I continued to fight. Jo had a big soft spot for me, and when Mum was too emotional to be with me, Jo would step in.

We were living at Ronald McDonald house, which was a place that undoubtedly saved my family much heartache, not to mention astronomical expense. The Ronald McDonald house kept us together, because there would have be no way my parents could have afforded to rent an apartment near the hospital on the days I was allowed to leave for just a day or two.

Late one night, I came down with a massive fever. Mum had no idea how to deal with a temperature of 41 degrees Celsius in an adult, let alone a small child. So, she did what she was told to do. She lay me in a bath of ice on top of a towel with a fan over me. Nevertheless, it just wasn't working. For whatever bizarre reason, late on that very night, Jo decided to come up to the house to visit me. She walked in, took one look at me, and she immediately took over.

She grabbed me, gave Mum the car keys, and we drove to the Oncology Ward. Jo actually had me hanging out of the car window in a desperate attempt to get my temperature down. That's when the febrile fit started. I used to have severe fits when I got high temperatures.

Yet within five minutes of nurse Jo taking over, it was all under control. Mum and I bonded so powerfully with Jo that we ended up moving in with Jo. During the hard times, if Mum didn't quite understand what the doctors were saying, she could speak to Jo about anything, regardless of the time.

Jo had a knack for putting all the medical jargon into layman's terms so that Mum could understand what was happening to me. It was understanding what was happening that helped her to get through it. Once Mum knew what the doctors were doing, she could accept it and follow through with their instructions. I truly believe that Nurse Jo saved our lives; one time in particular was after I had surgery.

I had gone seven hours without passing urine. Not passing urine can be a bad sign, because as the doctors told Mum, they had taken all of my organs out of my body and placed them all on a table during the surgery. The doctors removed as much of the cancer as they could, then they placed my organs back into my body, although I am sure it's far from as simple as it might sounds. Sometimes when vital organs are removed, the bladder can get twisted, which can stop you from urinating.

This is what the nursing staff thought must have happened. Fortunately for me, this happened at midnight. Jo was on oncology night duty that night, and Mum rang her to explain what was going on. Jo came straight over to Intensive Care, and she asked the sister whether she had tried everything to make me urinate. Jo once again just took over:

She grabbed me, took me over to the sink, and she put my feet under the running water. She splashed water all over me, and then the water fountain began. It's funny, because sometimes I still need to do this to help me go to the toilet.

I'll turn the tap on, and away it goes. Jo now has two beautiful children, and Mum and I are very proud to be their Godparents. Making us Godparents just shows so beautifully and powerfully the impact that Jo had on our lives for such a long time. Even when I go down to Sydney to have tests as an adult, I always stay with her.

Mum tells me stories about how she would have to attend death counselling once per week for two hours in order to deal with what they thought was going to happen to her son. She tells me a story about how she was lying in bed with me one day.

She was not allowed to touch me, because I was so badly burned. She said: "I remember this day like it was yesterday, Michael. You were lying next to me and you whispered to me. You said: "Mommy, I had a dream. My dream is, when I grow up, I want to be normal like everybody else."

I didn't tell my Mum that I wanted to be a professional athlete. I didn't tell her that I wanted to be a fireman or a police officer. I just wanted to be normal, like everybody else. I wanted to appreciate the finer things in life everyone else took for granted, such as going to school and making friends.

My Mum tells me that it broke her heart when she heard that, so she did something that the doctors told her not to do, and that was to pick me up. My skin was so badly burned that she wasn't permitted to hold me. What happened next changed my life forever. She leaned down into the bed to pick me up, because she desperately wanted to hold her little boy. She tore the skin off of my hands. She ripped out all my needles. She tells me through free-flowing, unchecked tears that on that day, she had tried so hard to take my pain away, but to her horror, she caused me much more pain .

I truly believe in my life that everything has happened for a reason. I can't speak for anybody else, but I reflect on my challenges and I know that every time I've been knocked- down, I've learned something important. Each time, I become stronger.

Each time, I become more determined. The needles could no longer go in my hand. So, they took the bandages off my head. They told my Mum to leave, which made me cry. I cried just long enough for the veins to pop out, and then, they inserted the needle into my skull to continue the treatment.

I could have complained because I had a needle in my head or I could rejoice in the simple fact that, for the first time in years, I had two free hands. It's not the adversity in our life that defines who we are; it's how we deal with our adversity that determines whether we lead remarkable lives. Life is all about choices. Every day, we are faced with choices that can reshape our tomorrows, and every day we are bestowed with the wonderful gift of the opportunity to enjoy today.

The drugs continued to burn long after. Lung infections continued for months and months. These infections just wouldn't go away. Then one day, I had a visit from the respiratory doctor. He asked Mum to go for a walk with him and she got some news. No matter what the news was, my Mum would always return to my room with tears in her eyes and say: "Everything is going to be fine, son".

I never told her that I could see in her eyes she was not telling the truth, but I always hoped that one day I could return her favour: If I ever had to hear the doctor tell me that my health was bad, then I was going to tell Mum that everything was going to be OK. Years later, I learned that the doctor had told Mum they were considering placing me on a lung transplant list because of the damage caused by the chemotherapy and the test drug.

Not only was it damaging my lungs, but it was damaging my heart as well. That was another hurdle. Mum looked at it as a hurdle. Mum asked whether there was any way that she could personally help the situation. To Mum's surprise, they asked Mum to get me to blow up balloons, blow bubbles with the bubble blower, and skip.

We continued to do this day after day, and I continued to take the antibiotics and medicines that the doctors prescribed. Then a miracle happened. Six months later, there was no need for a transplant. Someone upstairs was watching.

CHAPTER FIVE

DREAMS SAVE LIVES

"It's difficult to follow your dreams.
It's a tragedy not to." Ralph Marston

"Shoot for the moon. Even if you miss,
you'll land among the stars." Les Brown

"Don't be pushed by your problems.
Be led by your dreams." Ralph Waldo Emerson

After many months, the skin finally grew back on my hands. My Mum went out and she bought me a velcro glove and a velcro ball. She would sit at the end of my bed and lob the ball to me, and I'd catch it and throw the ball back.

She told me in later years that she would get farther and farther away until she'd be outside the hospital room; she'd be throwing the ball past the doctors and past the nurses, and I would give it my all to catch the ball. I recall thinking at the time that I was the best baseball player ever, because I never dropped the ball, although I realised when I got older that may have had something to do with the velcro.

I'd be in my room with the needle in my head, diving out of my bed, making the catch and trying to fire it back to her, past the doctors and nurses. When I started to get a little stronger and healthier, I would practice my sliding nearly every day; I'd run up and down the hallway and she'd run next to me with my trolley, the needle still in my head, and I'd be sliding into the base of the beds where Mum had piled loads of pillows to stop the ball travelling further. I would try to be as normal as I could, because this had been my first dream.

I tried to enjoy the little things that I was allowed to experience every day, whether it was sneaking outside for some fresh air without the nurses knowing, which made me feel very naughty, or waking up early to feel the warmth of the sun beaming through the hospital windows. Every night, I would go to bed and pray so hard that one day I was going to be allowed to go home to be with my family.

The cleaner always seemed keen to come into my room to clean my floor at 4:00am, which invariably woke me up. Once I was awake, I'd have nothing to do, so I would turn the TV on. Back in those days, the only television networks airing at that time of day were the ABC and another channel that played the major league baseball in America. After playing catch with my Mum and watching major league baseball on TV, all of a sudden I had another dream.

This dream was bigger then ever before; more sacrifices were needed and many laughs would be had by the sort of people who only ever tell you what you can't do in life. The dream was to one day play baseball in America.

Thinking back, I am glad that the only channels airing at that time back in those days were either the ABC or a sports channel, because I would hate to have turned on SBS at 4am in the morning. Who knows what my dream could have otherwise been? Ha ha!

I think that there is great wisdom in the expression: "Shoot for the moon. Even if you miss, you'll land among the stars."

If you have a dream, then you have a passion, a burning desire to see your dream come true. While you work towards the realisation of your dream, time goes by without you even noticing, work is something that you enjoy doing, and you forget the world around you. When you wake up in the morning, it does not matter whether it is a sunny or a rainy day. You see every new day as an opportunity to take you closer to your goal. What other people say or think about your dream becomes irrelevant.

You simply know that you're going in the right direction. Because you're inspired, you feel a constant flow of energy.

If you feel this way, you have defined your dream and maybe your destiny. The only other ingredient to fulfill your dream is persistence.

As we ride the planet around the sun, life can sometimes be hard and complicated. We dream of living better lives or achieving great goals. For many, the state of our present lives results from being born into difficult circumstances or surviving tragedies. Nevertheless, no matter where we find ourselves, our lives are also a reflection of all the choices we've made along the way.

It's crazy that some of the most powerful and influential people on this planet have faced true adversity and suffering throughout their upbringing. Still, these people never use that as an excuse to fail, but instead, they use their experiences to harness their burning desire to succeed.

I have witnessed too often people who are violent towards their partners or their children because their own parents behaved in the same manner when they were kids. I don't see that as an excuse for bad behaviour at all. Instead, sometimes your parents and other people of influence can actually set the behaviour that you should not follow. You actually learn from their mistakes and poor behaviour.

Yet, we still hear about people who overcame impossible odds to achieve great things in life. There are often tales of being at the right place at the right time, a coincidence, or meeting the right person just when they needed to.

Did the lucky few who made it just so happen to find Aladdin's magic lamp that delivered these miracles? How do the rest of us get one of those?

In my opinion, we all have a magic lamp. It is our unshakeable commitment to achieve our dreams. No matter where we find ourselves, I believe that this commitment is always inside and it is waiting to be tapped.

I was committed and wanted to be the person who did the 10% extra and then fell into the 1% category of achieving what many believed to be the impossible dream.

CHAPTER SIX

THE DAY THAT WAS NEVER TO HAPPEN

"When everything seems to be going against you,
remember a plane takes off against the wind, not with it."
Henry Ford

After many years of living in the hospital, the doctor finally said to my Mum the words that she prayed for, but never thought she would ever hear. "Kerri, take your boy home." The excitement and the emotions elicited by that simple statement were almost too much to handle; she let out an almighty cheer and the tears just flowed down her face as she squeezed me harder than I thought possible.

But, "Take your boy home" did not mark the end of the conversation. The doctor went on to say that due to the after-effects of all the drugs, I'd never go to school, I'd never play sport, I'd be a house-bound baby, and if I reached my teenage years, it'd be a miracle."

My Mum's heart sank, but she didn't allow it to sink for long because my Mum and my family had always believed in miracles, and she thought that this was just going to be another hurdle to deal with.

They had told her years before that I wouldn't make it to two-years-old, so who are they to tell her I wouldn't make it to 12?

Too often, we allow others to dictate our lives, but our family has always believed in our hearts that no human being determines when your life is up; God is the one in control.

My mum wanted my first dream to come true, which was to be normal like everybody else. She wanted to allow me to enjoy the simple things in life that so many of us just take for granted. So on Monday morning, straight out of hospital, she let me go to school like everybody else.

I imagined how school was going to be. I'd walk through the school gates. Everyone would be nice to me. I was going to make great friends. I was going to be the class clown. I was going to be the teacher's pet. Everyone was going to like me. Instead, I walked through the school gates and the school bully was there.

I've been called every name under the sun, including cancer boy, burnsy, odds-defier, baldy. I would be lying if I said that I didn't care. Mum used to tell me to remind myself of the saying: "Sticks and stones may break my bones, but names will never hurt me.", but that's not true; names absolutely do hurt you.

My time at school was tough. Really tough. I had imagined how it was going to be, and I was so wrong. I just wanted people to like me and be my friend.

I knew from a very young age that I was never going to be normal. Whilst all the other kids were out in the playground, I would sit in the classroom every recess and lunch on my nebuliser to give my lungs the strength to simply walk to the bus stop of an afternoon.

There were many lonely days at school ahead. I could easily complain that I was stuck inside a classroom feeling different, or I could be excited that I was not in hospital.

I think that it is so important in life that we realise that it's not our adversity that defines us, but rather, how we deal with it. I started to reflect on another saying my Mum often repeated.

She would say to me after a rough day at school: "Son, remember: What doesn't kill you only makes you stronger."

She was right; my Mum was always right. The names, the different way I looked, and the challenges I had faced didn't kill me, but boy did they make me stronger.

Even though there were so many dark days, I was never really alone; not only did I have my family and God who never left my side, there were also many different charities that supported me through thick and thin.

The charities that came into my life completely lifted me out of pain and adversity, and they led me to normality, joy, and happiness. One day, a lovely couple by the name of Tom and Nancy Strickland came into my life.

What an impact they had on our family's life! They were an absolute godsend. They came to the property one day. I was outside in the yard with Mum.

They introduced themselves to me, and they asked whether it would be at all possible for them to take me to a Camp. Mum thought she wouldn't let me leave her sight at any stage, so she immediately replied to them: "No." They said: "It's JUST one week a year; you deserve a break." All mum could say was: "I don't want a break. I just need to be with him."

They explained what Camp Quality was all about, using the words optimism and resilience. They explained that the supervision they had over kids on camp was incredible.

They described the purpose of Camp Quality, which is to create a better life for every child in Australia who is living with cancer . They explained that they are committed to delivering national programs that build resilience and optimistic behaviours for all children living with cancer in Australia.

They talked in-depth about the word optimism and the hard work they take on trying to spread positivity, hope and enthusiasm by the way they interact with other people.

They talked about how driven they are in regards to maintaining their integrity, and about how they encourage the development of trust through personal leadership. They said that they are always celebrating life, with every day being an adventure.

They went on to say that they pride themselves on their accountability, that they always accept responsibility for actions and results, and that they accept nothing but excellence from their teams, encouraging them to seek greatness in all that they do. So, Mum relented and let me go.

The first time I went to camp, Mum admits that she must have called every second hour to find out where I was and what I was doing. The camps continued every year, which was a massive thing for me and all of our family. It was the one week every year when Mum didn't have to worry about asking people for favours, because she didn't have to worry about me.

Their key motto is: "Laughter is the best medicine", and that's so true because we can either choose to frown at a situation, or we could laugh at it. We laughed. It was a really good feeling. I feel very privileged to remain heavily involved with Camp Quality. I have gone from a camper to a companion, and I am now the National Ambassador. It's a real honour.

Another organisation that was a huge support to my family and I is The Cancer Council, whose vision is to achieve a cancer-free future for the Australian community. With their mission in mind, they work with the community to reduce the incidence and the impact of cancer.

Their values are all about making a real difference. They seek to yield a major, positive impact on the lives of all Australians.

They never stop seeking to improve and innovate what they do, and they are prepared to take risks to achieve breakthrough results. They are passionate about their mission, and they maintain a deep value of the community and each other. They show empathy, respect, and they value all.

The Cancer Council holds a very special day, called Daffodil Day, and this was something that my family and I were heavily involved in right at the beginning. The daffodil has been recognised internationally as the symbol of hope for people in our community who have been touched by cancer, either directly or indirectly.

The daffodil heralds the beginning of spring, the season of hope, and the new life that it brings. It also reminds us that there is life after a diagnosis of cancer.

A lady from the United States offered to support our regional areas by bringing the flowers to our township so that we could do the best we could to sell them to raise money. I would go with my bald little head and my Camp Quality shirt to sell these beautiful flowers. The first year we sold every single flower.

The support and the money we made were overwhelming. What we realised at the end of the day is that everybody just wanted us to take the flowers home and to accept their money. "Give the flowers to your family", they would say.

Mum said it made her feel like the Mayor of Coffs Harbour. It was amazing: People whom I had neither met nor seen before in my life were so caring and so giving; it continued to give us hope.

By this stage, I had been home for some time now, and my family was trying to get my life back to normal, or as normal as what they could make it. I was about to celebrate my sixth birthday, and this was going to be the first birthday that I had ever celebrated at home, so you can imagine how excited I was.

Before we had left the hospital, the doctor had talked about my future and how it did not look bright. However, one thing that was emphasised to my Mum was to ensure that my stress levels were kept to an absolute minimum, because stress exerts a major influence on whether or not cancer returns.

Mum thought that she would throw on a surprise birthday party. I had come home from a day at the park after enjoying some good quality family time, when Mum asked me whether I would mind going to the garage to grab the broom.

I made my way down to the garage, and I opened the roller door. To my immense surprise, people jumped out of nowhere from behind the door, yelling: "Surprise! Happy Birthday!" I was so frightened that in front of all my family and friends, I soiled my underwear.

My mum immediately thought back to what the doctor said: "Do not stress him out", and she had just done exactly that.

She told me that I cried, although I think it was more with embarrassment than fear. After getting all cleaned up, I had a wonderful afternoon, and I enjoyed the best ice cream cake you have ever seen in your life.

Ah, the memories; I'm sure as I grow old, it will not be the last time I soil my pants.

CHAPTER SEVEN

HEART STOPPED AT AGE 12!!!!

"Sometimes you have to get knocked down lower than you've ever been, to stand up taller than you ever dreamed!" Anonymous

Another tremendous challenge for me as a child was the transition between primary school and high school. I went to a primary school with a total population of just twenty eight children. The school was in our small country village in Crossmaglen. Everyone knew everybody, and we only had one teacher who taught the entire school.

I graduated year six, and I headed off to high school. I attended Toormina High, where the total population of students was over 1200. The school had basketball courts, football fields, libraries, a massive hall, and different subjects were taught in different areas of the school. The drastic change in culture was extremely overwhelming, to say the least.

It was very challenging to venture into this massive school and to know nobody, besides my two older sisters who were still attending the school.

For the first month, I felt like a real loner; I would roam the hallways, walk out onto the football field, head past the basketballers, and even wander into the library, trying to find where I could fit in. Even the handball courts were so packed that I could barely get anybody's attention, let alone try to make a friend.

It was a really tough time. I had finally made some good, solid friends at my primary school, but they had all gone to a private high school. I was feeling very alone. I think when you get to that point in your life, you really stop seeing reality; you think people are saying things about you, but they're really not.

You even become a little bit paranoid, but I continued to remember that my life could be so much worse. So, I reminded myself that life had been so much tougher in the past, to just stay strong, and to do my best not to show any emotion, because one day things would get better. And things did get better in the most remarkable way.

It was week five of term one and I was walking through the hallway alone again when a young girl with Down Syndrome decided to start chasing me. I freaked out and ran as fast as I could until one of the boys in my year grabbed me, told me to hide under the seat, and said that he would cover the seat with school bags.

So, as he suggested, I jumped under the seat, and he and a group of other boys all sat in front of the bags. The girl just ran straight past us. When the coast was clear, I popped out from underneath the seat and the boys all introduced themselves to me. We all had a chuckle, and 18 years later, I'm still friends with those boys.

I was finally enjoying the life that I always wanted and never thought possible. I was finally at home with my family, I was finally making friends, and I was starting to live life on my terms. I was finally getting to play sport and loving the game of baseball, because I wasn't just playing it in hospital anymore; I was playing it for real.

We had a few challenges along the way, until one day the fear really set in. We would go down to Sydney every three months for tests, which were extremely taxing on the body, not to mention the family's finances.

One trip out of all these trips was expected to be just like all the others; I had to have a bone and gallium scan, ultrasounds, and CT scans. There were special diets and I had to fast for some of these tests. We were on the plane, and Mum had just got up to use the bathroom. The hostess was sitting there with me having a good old chat, and everything was fine.

We then got to the hospital. The radiologist started the first scan, and no sooner had they started the scan, they found a massive lump in my stomach. Obviously, everyone felt immense panic. Doctor Mary Bergin got called over to radiology, and they said: "It doesn't look good." That was Mum's greatest fear; that it would come back.

They had mentioned to Mum often throughout my treatment in previous years that even if I survived, the chance of recurrence is very high. Mum kept saying: "It can't be, Mary. It can't be; please say its not true".

Doctor Mary replied: "I can see it, Kerri. Has he eaten?" Mum snapped back: "No. He ate nothing."

Mum then said to me accusingly: "Did you eat anything Michael?"

I said: "Your chewing gum on the plane, Mum; I ate it all up."

That was the lump that everyone panicked about. It was a big wad of chewing gum in my stomach. I love my chewing gum. I still love my chewing gum. It is easy to laugh about it now, but my poor Mum nearly had a meltdown.

On our way home from hospital, my uncle who lived in Sydney, suggested that we catch up. He said, "Let's all meet up at McDonald's. We'll have lunch." When we got into McDonald's, there was a big picture on the wall of the actual Ronald McDonald House where we used to stay.

I was standing there, engrossed in the picture. The manager actually came up to us, and at this stage, I still didn't have any hair. The manager said to me: "That's an amazingly big house; isn't it?"

I replied: "No." The gentleman said: "What do you mean 'no'?" My comment was: "That house makes me sick." This poor guy had no idea what I was talking about. Then my uncle said: "Michael spends a lot of time at Ronald McDonald House."

He lifted my hat to show him my shiny head. The gentleman said: "You know what? It's a privilege to know someone that stays at that house. Let me buy you all lunch."

My impulsive response was: "We don't love your burgers. They're awful, but we like your ice creams." So, we all got an ice cream cone. Uncle Wayne wasn't happy. Ha ha.

When we arrived back home, I enjoyed playing the game that I loved. I was never the best player, but I always tried my best, and it took me until my 12th birthday for me to reach the level of representing my hometown of Coffs Harbour. We went away to the country championships where they selected the top 16 players to represent New South Wales, and I can't begin to tell you how excited I was to make that team.

However, one week before we were due to fly out to the national championships, I became very unwell, and I was taken to hospital. I was told by the doctors I had Glandular Fever, and whilst I was in hospital, I managed to catch even more viruses due to my low immune system. Then, my entire world changed forever.

I had four doctors on my left and my mother holding my hand on my right, where she has always been, and I went to take a deep breath in. The pain in my chest is something that's almost impossible to describe: the agony, the suffering, the sharpness, and the intensity of the pain was mind-blowing.

At the age of 12, I had suffered my first major heart attack and my life was never going to be the same. Mum was petrified. She was actually asked to leave the room. She said she was behind the curtain; there was no way she was leaving the room. She said she stayed beside me while they did what they had to do. I heard them say: "Clear."

That was when Mum realised that they were using those paddles on me. She burst out crying and thought to herself: "Why? Not again. Please don't take him from me." A short time passed, which Mum said felt like days, and she heard me talking with the doctors.

That was when they discovered how much heart damage I had sustained from the cancer treatments. Again, we didn't let that beat us. I often say that I have a VIP card to hospitals.

I never get a free coffee or a stamp on my hand, but they certainly all knew me and treated me well. The feeling of being helpless is something that registers in my heart and my mind when I hear about these situations, because I think it's a really powerful exercise to step out of your own shoes and look at life through someone else's eyes.

Throughout the really tough times it would have been so hard for my Mum. It would have been so difficult having a big family, with Dad taking care of the girls, although it was difficult to have all of my sisters with me because my parents didn't really want them to understand the severity of what I was going through.

All they ever wanted was for me to come home. That was my therapy. I used to even say to the doctors: "Let me go home, Doctor. I'll get better." Nine times out of 10 I did.

I was in hospital for many months and missed so much school, but my Mum being who she is, never allowed me to feel sorry for myself, and she never allowed me to fall behind. So, she would have teachers come in every second day with schoolwork to ensure that I didn't miss out on learning. I was fortunate that year to be dux of my class, so I didn't need to repeat that year.

When I was finally allowed to go home, the doctor said something that really challenged me. He told me that I would never play sport again and that I must be very careful about how hard I exercised as the strain on my body and my heart had been immense.

Nevertheless, I love it when people tell me what I can't do, because it makes me work very hard to show them that I can. I'm never out to prove other people wrong, but I just enjoy working hard every day to prove myself right. "Can't" is a word that shouldn't be a part of anyone's vocabulary.

I refuse to believe that things can't be done. Have you ever noticed that some people are sometimes a little too quick to tell you why something can't be achieved?

When someone mentions the word "can't", it might be about embarking on a type of project you've never done before, creating a new product, launching into a new country, applying for a great new job or winning a battle that CAN'T be won.

Can't is a word used by people who are just projecting their own fears out into the world, by people who can't see past their present limitations, and by people who don't realise that given the right mentality, they too, can begin manifesting their dreams at a rapid pace. It's much easier to make excuses not to do something big and overwhelming than to simply put one foot in front of the other to start chipping away at the not-so-glamorous work of making your dreams come true.

Why do people do that?

I think that people are just so scared of making a mistake. It's a fear of failure, and a fear of embarrassment. Maybe they're fearful of change. I think it's a completely normal and healthy human response to feel all of these things when embarking into the unknown and when taking risks. But if you recognise that this fear is just a passing emotion that doesn't necessarily have to chain you into not making any moves, then you might be able to set yourself free.

Miracles are just a shift in perception from fear to love. For some people, it's just safer to do nothing rather than try something new. They can maintain the status quo. They don't want to rock the boat. They're in their comfort zone. But, life only really begins at the end of your comfort zone. It's overwhelming to imagine what a different world we would be living in if everyone listened to those who said it can't be done. It used to be thought that it was not humanly possible to run a mile in less than four minutes.

Yet, Roger Bannister broke the four-minute barrier with a time of 3:59.4. Soaring through the air in a flying machine? Can't be done, said the skeptics, including the Wright Brothers' own father who scoffed at the idea, saying that they should leave flying to the birds. Going into space? Can't be done. Can't is an ugly word. It should be banished from our thoughts. Mindset is everything.

By simply making some minor adjustments to how we think and by removing the negative thoughts we tell ourselves, which leave us ruled by fear, we can make great strides towards our desired end result.

Anything is possible if you have a clear vision and are willing to do the work. I've never accepted that I can't accomplish what I set out to do. There's simply no room for "can't" in my life.

Henry Ford's quote is so apt in capturing this point: "Whether you think you can or think you can't—you are right". Whenever I've been told that something is impossible or something simply can't be done I just smile, and deep down inside, I say to myself: "Just watch me."

CHAPTER EIGHT

BLOOD, SWEAT AND TEARS

*"Adversity causes some men to break,
others to break records."* William Arthur Ward

*"Have a goal each day to create the kind of self that you will be happy
to live with for the rest of your days."* Michael Crossland

I had created a dream and a vision, so I needed to get out of my comfort zone and go out into this world and make it happen.

It's amazing what can be achieved when you can imaginatively extend yourself beyond what previously seemed impossible. By going deeper, and by doing so, understanding yourself better, you create a better balance. The heart and soul are enhanced.

Then, you become more focused on the positive. Most people are focused on what they believe they "can't" do, and not on what they "can" do. Fear is the paralysis and usually the culprit that knocks you down and holds you down to make you quit; I was never going to quit. I was going to live my life on my terms and make it happen, not let it happen.

I kept playing baseball, even though I was told not to, but I played a little smarter. I made sure that I never overdid it. I made sure I always warmed-up adequately. I made sure I always warmed down properly.

I wasn't the fastest, or the biggest, or the strongest, but I knew the game inside and out. I love the game. I just wanted to get better. I wanted to always try a little harder than everybody else.

I always wanted to make sure that I did the 10 percent extra every time my coach asked me to do something. I wanted to make sure that I did that little bit more to not merely catch up with the others, but to leap frog ahead of them at one stage in my life. I really wanted to make sure that I consistently did the 10% extra that allowed me to fall into the 1% category who manage to fulfill their dreams.

I remember there was one man who was around throughout my childhood; he was very involved with baseball on a local level, and he used to always tell me that I was far too small to play baseball, and that I would never make it in this game.

Little did he know that was all the fuel I needed to doggedly pursue my dreams. It took me until the age of 15 to get myself to the level I needed to be to, once again, represent my town of Coffs Harbour. I played so well at a tournament that I was selected to play for the New South Wales State Team.

As fortune had it, one afternoon after the tournament was finished, I got a tap on the shoulder by a man who would change my life forever. His name was John Murray. At that time, he was the head coach and tour manager of Brisbane Expo's touring baseball team. They went to America once per year for three weeks, and they travelled around the country and played 15 games of baseball.

He told me that the program was not about taking amazing athletes to America; instead, it was far more forward- thinking than that.

The tour was based around what he referred to as "the A Principal", which was an acronym for Attitude, Ability and Achievements. The key word was Attitude. The day that he told me that I was in the team was the day I realised that my dream was only just around the corner from coming true. The clincher was that it was very expensive. It was $5,000.

My family have never had money, so it was going to be a big challenge for me to get there.

I always wanted to do things off my own bat. We had to train every weekend in Brisbane and there was no way that we could afford the flights up and back all the time. I would play Saturday morning in Coffs Harbour, and then I would get on the 4:30pm Greyhound bus to Brisbane.

I would get to Brisbane at 12:30am, just after midnight. John, my coach, would pick me up, and we'd go back to his house. I'd fall asleep for a few hours, then wake up in the morning, have breakfast and head to Redlands Baseball field.

We trained from 9am until 5pm, and then I would head back into the city. I'd have some dinner with him and he'd put me on the 8:30pm bus home.

I would get to Coffs Harbour at 4:30 Monday mornings. My Mum or Dad would come down to pick me up from the highway and drive me back up out to Crossmaglen.

I would then shower, have some breakfast, put my school clothes on, go to bed for an hour or so, and then get back up to walk the 1.2 kilometres to the end of the road to get the school bus back to school.

If ever I missed a Monday morning of school, I wasn't allowed to go to training the following week. That was the deal that my Mum and Dad had set with me. My studies were never going to be negatively impacted by playing the game that I loved.

I never missed one weekend of training because I never missed a Monday morning of school. Mum never realised that I may have spent a few Monday mornings in the sick bay to get some rest. Ha ha.

I had to make sure that I came up with the bus money every week on my own though. Not only did I have to raise the $5,000 that I needed to get myself to America, but I also needed to raise the $80 per week to get on the bus.

I would do pretty much anything in hard labour to make that money. I would wash cars and weed driveways. I remember spending a lot of time with one of my coaches, Kerry Owen, who lived out at Crossmaglen.

I would mow his lawns, wash his cars, pick up palm fronds, and pick fruit for him. I would do whatever it took to make sure I got the $80 to get me on that bus so I could get out and learn, really hone in my skills, and nurture the talent that god had given me, so I could continue to get better and compete.

I remember one day I was knocking on doors asking whether I could do some yard work to raise the money I needed, and I finally managed to get inside the door of a really rich couple. They had the most beautiful home and they had all the fancy cars.

They finally agreed that I could help them out around their home, so they asked me to weed their driveway, which must have been at least 100 meters long. It took me nearly eight hours, and I was exhausted after a huge day, bending at the hips to pull out weeds.

When it finally came to pay day, he said to me that I had done a fantastic job. He handed me an envelope and said: "Thanks for your effort." I could not wait to leave the property so I could rip open the envelope to see how much cash had been stuffed in there.

I ran down his driveway, and when I was out of sight, I stopped to open the envelop. Inside the envelope were two $5 notes. I had worked nearly 8 hours and he had paid me $10. I couldn't believe it; I was thinking that I had probably made enough for at least one week's worth of bus trips. I felt momentarily angry, but after a little while, I laughed it off and and thought: "Only $70 to go."

The $5,000 to get me on that plane wasn't easy either. It was a hard slog. Raising that money meant lots of raffles, trivia nights, auctions, and fundraising, but I managed to get there thanks to the generosity of the local community.

I must have knocked on every single business door in Coffs Harbour, saying: "Please, can you donate something? Let me buy something off you at cost price, and try to either give it away in a raffle, or auction it off to get me over to America."

The support that I received was unbelievable. I feel so privileged and blessed to have had them along as part of that journey. I guess that made that milestone of playing baseball in America that much more worthwhile because nothing was ever handed to me, and nothing was just given to me. It was hard work, determination, commitment, and the inner belief that I was going to get there, which allowed me to achieve it.

Sadly, these days, its almost an expectation that people are handed everything for nothing, including not only what they need, but also everything they want. In my opinion, this instills a complete lack of appreciation for anything, and the hard work needed to achieve anything is just disregarded.

The auctions were done, the raffles were finished, and the fundraising was over. The grand total amount raised was $5530. I was over the moon, because I was going to America, and I had spending money.

My doctors were concerned about me flying for such lengthy periods of time because my immunity was still poor. I had to pack what looked like a lifetime supply of medication and vitamins, and I was ready to go. I was really focused on how hard I had trained and what I was eating, so that I could be as fit and as healthy as possible.

The weekend prior to departure we were given our uniforms; I cried when I received my jersey with my special number on the back. It had the name, CROSSLAND, with the number 24, in large, bold, black print.

Very few people that day realised why I was so emotional and why that number meant so much to me. You see, I never played by myself when I was wearing that number; I was always playing for the 24 little angels who did not make it through that horrible test drug.

John, my coach, told me that he knew why I was in tears, and he held me like I was his own son. He said that he was so proud of me and the determination that I had shown.

He asked me what I wanted to achieve whilst I was in America. I responded with a clear answer: "I just want to turn a double play in the States."

I realised at training that I was never going to be the biggest, the strongest, the guy that was going to be the starting shortstop, the superstar, or the guy whom they relied on to make sure that we could win or compete as effectively as we could. These guys were just giving me an opportunity, because I had a little bit of talent, a big heart and a massive dream.

The day had finally come when I had to say goodbye to my family, and then, I was up and away. I think I packed four weeks early, because I was so excited. My Mum cried, and I think she cried for many reasons.

It was not just that she was going to miss her boy. I think she was also reflecting on the past and thinking to herself: "How has this happened? My little boy, who was not supposed to make his 2nd birthday, is now a young man and he is heading to America to live his dreams."

I think this point in my life was truly a defining moment. It proved to me and my family that anything is possible if you work hard and dream big. I remember flying into LA feeling exhausted but excited as I looked out the window and saw baseball fields everywhere, tall buildings, and eight lane highways.

We got off the plane, and we headed through customs, wearing the biggest smiles on our faces. We headed outside to get on the bus, and we all looked the wrong way, because the cars came flying past us on the wrong side of the road!

I remember getting into the hotel room and needing to go to the toilet after all of the fantastic plane food. I finished doing my business and flushed the toilet; I was immediately frightened, because the toilet started filling up, as in, the contents were getting closer to the top, rather than disappearing!

I yelled at my roommate, and he started laughing uproariously; he was a veteran traveler, so he knew exactly what was going on. The toilet eventually began to suck the water back, and its contents finally went down with it. It had me panicking for a moment there.

It was time for game one. We listened to our national anthem, the Australian flag was being raised, and as I ran out onto the baseball field, I heard my name announced through the PA: "From Coffs Harbour, New South Wales number 24, Michael Crossland". I had goosebumps, and tears streamed down my face.

The sacrifices were worth it. The dedication and discipline were worth it.

The commitment had all been worth it, because I had achieved something that people told me all my life I would never ever be able to achieve. It was late in the game when I played second base. My dream of turning a double play became a reality.

It was the game ending double play, and I had not realised that John (our coach, who went by the name JM) had told the rest of the team about my dream.

They hoisted me onto their shoulders and allowed me to bask in my moment in the sunshine. I think that nothing is impossible when you want to fulfill a dream. Many people will tell you that you can't do it, and that you don't have what it takes, but if it is in your heart and you feel it, there is nothing that will stop you.

I remember going into a town called Redlands and meeting some of the most amazing people that you could ever meet in your life. These people weren't just there for an hour. They weren't there just for a week. I knew that these people were going to be a part of my life forever.

The man who ran the American side of this baseball program was named Steve Chapman, and boy did we become life-long friends! Through JM, they had found out a little of my story, and Steve had a list of people a mile long whom he wanted me to meet.

The list included Chris McPeck, Michael Ramos, and Dennis Craig, and these introductions continued until we headed to lunch with a family who touched my heart; it was the Flanigans.

They arrived in my life and immediately entered my heart with their kindness, love, support and other amazing human qualities that I wanted to emulate.

There are just some people in your life who come in the front door, shut it behind them, and throw away the key. They were to be a part of my life forever more.

I remember staying with a family called the Hausos. Their son, Christopher, was the second baseman for the American team, and I was the second baseman for the Australian team.

Not only did we become friends, we became best mates to the point that he was in my wedding party nearly ten years later. I quickly began to realise that this baseball program was far more than just a tour where young athletes get a chance to play baseball. This was a tour about life, about friendship, and about bringing people from other parts of the world together.

My return from my first trip to America with the Expos marked an epoch in my life. I felt as though I had returned home as a young man; I was not a little boy anymore. I was of the conviction that anything was possible, and I began to feel very confident in my own skin and in my own ability. My friendships at school had begun to blossom, and I was at a point in my life where I was just so happy and so content in the life that I was in.

I remember building up to the year 10 formal, which is a very big event on any high school student's social calendar. It was all about impressing, looking your best and having a great time. I remember asking one particular girl whether she would be my date for the formal. When she said yes, I was absolutely delighted.

The next day, she asked me whether her friend could join us. My immediate thought was: "How good is it going to look to the boys when I show up with two girls?"

A few days later, I remember hearing that another girl didn't have a date for the formal, so I decided to ask the two girls whom I was taking whether she could join us for an hour.

The girls said they were happy for this to happen. So, my year 10 formal was going to be an absolute beauty. I had organised a nice hire suit, my aunt was going to drive us in a fancy car, and we were going to get plenty of photos when I showed up to the formal with my three ladies.

Two days prior to the formal, I got very unwell and was bedridden, but I was going to make sure that I had the energy to attend the formal. I remember getting out of bed late in the afternoon that day, putting on my suit, and driving to pick up the girls. We went to the headland and got some photos, and later, we arrived at the venue for a few more photos.

We walked up the stairs to greet a few people, but I then took the exit door straight outside to get into the car to head home as my body would not let me keep going. I desperately needed more rest.

It would have been an amazing night with the rest of my classmates, but at least I managed to show up, make an entrance and get some photos, and I got a few brownie points from the boys, because I showed up with three girls.

Whilst I was in year 10 I was lucky enough to do work experience as a bellman at the Ritz-Carlton hotel in Sydney with my lifelong friend Wayne. He had worked there for many years and was able to open up some doors (pardon the pun) and give me this opportunity. I remember taking people's bags to their rooms, opening doors and receiving tips from rich businessmen. One day I remember Greg Norman was staying and he gave me $20 to go to his penthouse and grab him 4 VB's as the restaurant didn't serve that type of beer. Those 2 weeks of work experiences really shifted my mindset and I thought to myself, one day I don't won't to be the guy that opens the door and receives the tips, I want to be the guy that has my door opened for me and for me to be in a position to give the tips.

I was very pleased to make the Expos baseball team for the next two consecutive years, and it was truly was a dream come true each year to be a part of this program. This game wasn't just a sport to me. It wasn't just something that we did on the weekend.

It really became my life. These people in this Expo community were going to continue to help me live that dream.

I was 17 and had just finished my senior year at High School and was still passionate about living the dream of playing baseball in America. Money had always been tight in our family and if I wanted to play overseas I needed to pay my own way. My uncle Wayne Hosier ran an indoor air purification company selling the best vacuums on the planet. He offered me a role doing door to door sales, selling these $5500 vacuums. It was a commission only role, so the harder I worked the more money I made. He made a deal with me when I started that if I could sell 3 machines in a week he would give me his beautiful Statesman to drive around for the weekend. I worked very hard, not only to sell and save but to also get the opportunity to drive that car. Let's just say my uncle didn't have his car very often on weekends ha ha. My time in Sydney living with my uncle and auntie and working with them was fast paced, extremely long hours but I thoroughly enjoyed the challenge and boy did I make some money.

Just before my 18th birthday I was selected once again to play with the Expo's in the United States. I was fortunate to play baseball down in Texas. A scout by the name of John Lee said to me in his thick, Southern accent:

"Son, you ain't the biggest ball player I have ever seen, but that passion you have certainly shines through. I want to give you an opportunity to come to Texas and play some college ball."

I didn't know whether to cry or scream. I couldn't wait to get to a phone and call Mum to tell her what I thought was great news.

The phone call that I made that night was probably one of the toughest calls for me to make at this time in my life. She was pumped to hear my voice, but she was not so pumped to hear what I had to say.

I said to her: "Guess what, Mum? I am not coming home. I have been offered a scholarship to live here in Texas to play baseball for a college and also get an education." Mum's heart was so torn; she wanted her boy to come home, but she also wanted me to live my dream. Parents who truly love their children will move mountains and sacrifice their own yearnings and wishes in order to see their children live their dreams.

It's funny, because you move from Australia, where you're this little red-headed, skinny, freckly guy, and I've got a pretty awesome scar from where I got the cancer cut out.

None of the girls really wanted to talk to me back in Australia, and then, all of a sudden, I went to America and I spoke with a funny accent, and I suddenly became really good-looking; my new-found confidence and my accent no doubt blurred their vision somewhat. I've got to tell you, I didn't tell anybody in Texas that I'd been sick.

You can imagine the stories that I made up about that scar because, in Texas, when you talk, people invariably say to you: "Boy, you've got a funny accent. Where are you from?" I'd reply, "I'm from Australia, mate." You say it as fast as you can so no one has a clue what you said.

They'd say, "Australia? Nope, I've never heard of Australia. What state is Australia in?" You can tell them anything and they would believe you. I told them that my scar was from a mistimed jump off a paddle boat with Uncle Steve Irwin, which landed me on a crocodile's tail that cut me open. We would laugh and tell some wonderful stories.

They would believe me when I told them that I rode a kangaroo to school. My life was amazing; each morning I was so excited to simply get out of bed. I would sometimes pinch myself and think: "Is this really happening to me?" I was making great friends, I was playing great baseball, and I was feeling so blessed to have the life that I had.

I had never wanted people to know about my health, because I never wanted to be treated any differently from the others. But, like everything in life, you can reach a pinnacle, and it can all get taken away from you in a heartbeat. One bad choice, one bad decision ,or even a phone call, and your life can change forever. I was 18-years- old and I was certainly living the dream.

One day, I was playing a game in Arizona on a very hot Thursday night; the temperature was around 44 degrees Celsius at 8pm. I slid into second base and I woke up three days later in hospital. My health was deteriorating, my immune system was getting weaker, and I suffered even more heart challenges.

My dreams that I had worked so hard for came to an end. My dreams of playing baseball in America were over.

Three weeks after getting out of the hospital, I was on the plane heading home. It took me 44 hours to get back to Coffs Harbour, and I promise you, I cried 40 of those 44 hours, thinking that my life wasn't fair.

I thought: "How many times do I need to get knocked and kicked?" I felt like I was depressed, but there was this little feeling inside my heart of knowing that everything happens for a reason, and I was so excited to see my Mum.

I had no idea how much I would miss her, and I had forgotten the enormous comfort she brings to me when time gets tough.

When I landed in Coffs Harbour, I remember getting off the plane, and thinking to myself that I had two choices. I could get off the plane and let everybody know that my dreams had been crushed.

Everyone would have understood it. They would have appreciated it.

I could have got the sympathy vote for as long as I wanted it, or I could get off that plane with my head held high, knowing that I'd been able to achieve something far greater than what so many people thought I'd ever be able to achieve.

I got off the plane, with the biggest smile on my face, and my tiny chest was puffed out, because I was proud of what I'd been able to do. There were two TV reporters there to greet me. The first reporter was from A Current Affair.

The reporter said: "Mike, we want to do a story about your life. We think it's unfair what happened to you. We're going to do a 3-minute story about your life." Then she said that they would pay me $30,000 to do it.

I didn't care whether it was 30 seconds. I was an 18-year-old boy, with a large medical bill in American to pay, and I had no job and no car. I'd already picked out the car I was going to buy with my $30,000.

Fast and the furious was the fashion in cars back in those days. It was going to be a VN Holden Commodore Club Sport. It was going to lowered, have 18-inch rims, neon lights underneath, and the boot was going to have the biggest speaker that you've ever seen.

I wouldn't be able to fit my putter in there, let alone my golf bag. I was going to drive down the main street in the middle of winter, heater on, windows down, music pumping. I was going to be the biggest bogan in Coffs Harbour. Life was going to be awesome.

Then I got approached by another TV program at the same time. They said: "Michael, we want to do a 30-minute story about your life. We're from Australian Stories. We want to give you an opportunity to give back and make a difference."

A Current Affair were offering $30,000 for three minutes.

So, I am sure you can imagine what I was thinking: I just carried the zero to make it 30 minutes, and came to the logical amount of $300,000. How good is this going to be? I've gone from a VN Commodore to a Mercedes Benz. I've gone from 18-inch to 20 inch rims.

I wasn't going to be just a bogan anymore; I was going to be a rich bogan. I was going to look after my Mum. Life was going to be amazing.

I said: "How much?" They said: "Here, at Australian Stories, we don't pay for our programs. We do something far greater than that." That's when the 18-year-old brain pretty much switched off. I didn't care what they had to say; all I was thinking of was the car.

At that time, I was heavily involved with Camp Quality. There was a man from all those years ago who was still standing by my side, my dear friend and still head of Camp Quality in my area, Tom Strickland. He said to me: "Michael, here's your opportunity to give back. Here's your opportunity to make a difference in other people's lives as opposed to just trying to gain for yourself."

So, that's what I did. I'm so blessed and so privileged to have been a part of the Australian Story program, called Field of Dreams.

I remember day one of the filming. The camera crew arrived at my family home. They were all so kind and so caring and a bond was immediately formed. I remember the lady so clearly; her name was Janine Hoskins, and she said that she and her colleagues were so excited to be able to share my wonderful story.

We remain friends to this day, and I think that it was not so much my story but the way she produced it and shared it, that made it such a great success. They followed me around for weeks and filmed some of my day-to-day routine, which included training and and other activities, such as visits to the doctor and hospital.

I remember listening in my room one day as they interviewed my Mum, and they asked her to recall my time as a child and the challenges that she faced. I remember sitting there listening so intently as tears flowed down my face; it broke my heart listening to the pain and the suffering that she went through watching me have my treatment, and hearing how she felt so helpless and just wanted to take my pain away every day, but simply couldn't do anything to help.

She shared some of her stories that she would write in her diary every day. I walked in her shoes just for an hour throughout that interview and I learnt so much, not only about myself and my story, but also about the courage, the determination and her absolute refusal to ever quit on her little boy.

Somehow, that day my love, respect and admiration for my Mother peaked at an all-time high, and I was so grateful for everything she had done and the sacrifices that she had made.

To be told, over and over again, to just walk away and quit, but to still keep fighting, was so admirable. I can only think how difficult she would have been to all the nurses just by never taking no for an answer. I am so glad she didn't.

It was even amazing listening to my three sisters share how it was for them and the challenges they went through with not only having their brother away for so long, but more importantly, not having their Mum there with them as they grew from little girls into young teenagers.

It was an emotional roller-coaster, but it had certainly become an exciting one, because we were finally all home together, and we shared some wonderful memories and crazy stories.

CHAPTER NINE

SO BEGAN MY CAREER OR WAS IT

"We were given two ends, one to sit on and one to think with.
Success depends on which one you use the most." Ann Landers

"Dreams always come a size too big so we can
grow into them." Josie Bissett

"People can run a long way on just
a little encouragement." Hebrews 3:13

"Even when you think you have your life all mapped out,
things happen that shape your destiny in ways
you never imagined." Deepak Chopra

After the Australian Story aired on national TV, life became exciting for me. Lots of people started to recognise me when I walked down the street; many of them approached me, and asked to get their photo taken with me. I was asked to attend different events and share a little of my journey. I remember one company flew me in a private plane to their conference on the Gold Coast to sit and do a Q&A with their attendees.

But it did not last forever: The hype gradually faded, and at that stage, I was really a little lost. I had no job, no career, and no real direction. I managed somehow to start dating a young girl who was a cheerleader/dancer, so I thought I was "the man". I then moved to Newcastle and I got a job in finance, which was an industry I thought was awesome at the time. That career consumed me for many years.

At first, I got a job as the guy who stands at the front of the bank and welcomes you when you walk in. I had no idea about anything. My answer to every single question to every single customer was: "Yeah; no problem. Just make your way over to the teller and they'll be able to help you out." Whether the customer wanted a term deposit, a new account, or something else, my response was always: "Make your way over to the tellers and they will be able to help you out."

I gradually worked my way up into a position as a lender, and I began to learn very quickly that the more effectively you communicate, and the stronger the relationships you build, and the greater the amount of products you can sell.

I truly believed in what I was offering; I felt that I was helping people to get closer to their dreams, get them out of jams, and I was even putting them in a better financial position. It's amazing what happens when you really believe in a product; then, it really does sell itself.

I was building a great name for myself in the finance sector. I was the leader of all internal competition, I was making good money, and I had made some really great friends who became life-long friends. Baseball competition was solid in the Newcastle area. I had a great team that was very competitive, and life was rolling along smoothly.

One day a man came into my work and greeted me. He said his name was Tom, and he even addressed me by my name. I was pretty impressed that he knew my name, but then I realised that I was wearing a name badge. I replied: "Yes?" He said: "I'm the CEO; lets have a chat."

I went into the back room to get him a coffee, and on my way out there, I asked a female colleague who Tom was. She informed me that he was the CEO. I had no idea what a CEO was, so I asked her to explain what he did.

She informed me that CEO stands for Chief Executive Officer, which just made me even more confused, so I asked what that title meant, and she explained that he was the boss's boss's boss's boss. I thought to myself: "This guy must be rich, and I really need to impress him." So, I sat down, and I was feeling a bit nervous all of a sudden, because Tom was the big boss.

He said to me: "Michael, where do you see yourself in five years?" I was 19. All I cared about at that stage was where I was on a Friday night. I didn't care where I was going to be in five years. I didn't even know where I was going to be tomorrow.

I said to myself: "Could I be cheeky here and get away with it? Let's have a crack." So, I replied: "Tom, I'm going to work hard over the next five years, and I am going to take your job."

He looked at me thoughtfully: "Michael, I don't know whether you're arrogant or determined, but only time will tell." That's when my 19-year-old self should have shut-up, but my response to that was: "Yes; you're right, Tom. Only time will tell."

We didn't really get off on the right foot, but we eventually became good mates.

Within 12 months, I was a 20-year-old branch manager. This had its challenges, because my girlfriend and I were living in Newcastle and this role was a two and a half hour drive north to Port Macquarie.

I started the role whilst still living in Newcastle; I left home at 5:30am every day, and arrived close to 8am. I would work all day trying to impress my staff who were not only much more experienced then I was, but they possessed a far greater knowledge of both the industry and the area.

I would then drive home each afternoon, settling back into our home close to 8:30pm. I understood the sacrifices that were required to get ahead in life.

My family never had money, could never afford to go on holidays or drive a nice car, and we would never have a fancy meal out and about. I really wanted these things for my future family: I wanted to be the provider, and I wanted nice cars and a nice house, but in retrospect, I think that I really just wanted the perception that people paint of success.

With all of the travel and the pressure of getting the branch in a very lucrative position, I needed to commit more time to my work, which meant not driving home each day.

So, I started driving up on Mondays, travelling home on Wednesday nights, driving back up on Thursdays, and then driving home on Fridays for the weekend. This worked better, but it was still starting to strain the body and the mind.

Throughout this period of my life, I was still experiencing plenty of personal challenges, and my sister was separating from her husband. Then something happened that completely shattered my heart, and still shatters my heart to this day. My parents separated; they became one of the 80 plus percent of separated parents of children with cancer.

My Mum was heartbroken; she was so lost, and she was really struggling to find her purpose. It's truly awful when you see someone that you care about in so much pain, and there is nothing that you really can do to support her or take her pain away.

It made me reflect on the pain she must have felt watching me battle for so long.

With all that was going on at home with my family and the struggles at work, the stress to my already beaten body was just too much to handle, and I was rushed to hospital with an illness that they could not identify.

After seven lumber punctures over seven days, they transferred me from Maitland hospital to the John Hunter Hospital. I was put in the Palliative Care Unit as this was the only ward that had a free room that was isolated. You can imagine the fear on beautiful Nurse Jo's face when she called to check in on me only to find that I was in the Palliative Care Unit.

She hung the phone up and immediately drove from Sydney straight to Newcastle. Jo arrived and simply did what Jo does best. She made things happen. Finally, 24 hours after nurse Jo arrived, I was diagnosed with Bacterial Meningitis.

I had a large amount of fluid on the brain, and I had never felt so sick with so little energy and so much pain. It was a long stint in hospital, and yet again, the frustration of being stuck in the same bed, eating the same food, and having no choice about how to organise my days, started to build up.

I was very fortunate to have some great friends who would visit me in hospital every day. Brad Garland, my baseball mate, would bring me food, magazines, and plenty of laughs to lift my spirit.

My coach at the time, Nick, and his lovely wife would visit every second day. He owned several fruit shops, and each time they would bring a punnet of strawberries; they would have this big smile on their faces when they said: "We brought you strawberries." I didn't have the heart to tell them that I didn't like strawberries, but the nurses and doctors loved them.

I finally got out of hospital, and I tried to hit the ground running. Very quickly, I began to realise that the life I was living, the hours at work, and the challenges with my family, were taking a huge toll on my relationship with Renee, and after many years together, we went our separate ways. I recall many nights of tears, feeling so alone, and I questioned why all of these things were happening to me all at once.

But, I truly believe that we are tested every day, and with great adversity comes not only great strength, but also new ideas and opportunities.

Several months after getting back on my feet, I was promoted to the largest and most under-performing site in the country. I was moving to Parramatta, in the big smoke, and this was an opportunity to put the past behind me and to work hard to get to the top of the corporate ladder. But I did not go there alone; my angel came with me.

Let me take you back to when I had just returned home from the States from a baseball tour when I was 17. My angel entered my world at a young age, even though at the time, I had no idea of the impact she would have on my life.

She was at an auction with her father and I don't know why I was there, but as I wandered through all of the items that were up for auction, I saw a beautiful young girl walk past me. Her hair was flying in the wind.

Her smile instantly brought warmth and joy into my life. I remember she walked past and I said: "Hello". She said "Hi" back and we started chatting. It felt so comfortable, so right, so real. At this time, I didn't know how old she was. I just thought that she was beautiful.

I remember going home that afternoon and saying to my sister: "I met an angel today". She said to me: "Did you get her number? I said that I didn't know why I didn't get her number, but I didn't get her number. About two weeks later, I received a phone call from an unknown number, and she said: "Hi; it's Mel. I met you at the auction."

I was so delighted and so excited to hear her voice, because I couldn't track her number down, but she had tracked mine. I immediately arranged to catch-up with her for lunch on a Sunday and we had an amazing afternoon of chatting and laughing before I drove her home. When I dropped her off she said to me: "Would you like to pick me up from school tomorrow?" I said that I would love to.

In the back of my mind I was interested to know how old she was, purely because she was still at school. I was 17 and I thought she would be close to 17. I picked her up the next day from school and her uniform was a junior uniform, which as you can imagine, surprised me a lot, because I thought she was at least a senior.

Long story short, I found out that she was only in Grade 9 and she was 14. We stayed friends for a very long time. In fact, for six or seven years we stayed friends until our lives eventually came together once more, and not only were we friends, but we became soul mates. Our lives connected again. She made the first move with me and have been inseparable ever since.

So we embarked on this exciting journey together: She knows all of my stories, my challenges, and she is willing to make the best of the life we have. We made some amazing friends throughout our time in Sydney. We, like all couples, had our ups and downs, but she always supported me with everything that I embarked on.

Times were really challenging in the business world; the branch was under-performing, we had the wrong people working for the organisation, and I had to let a lot of people go. I think that the success of any business comes from its people, not its customers. The customers will come if you can create a great environment with products that you believe in.

I needed to have the right people in the right roles, and boy did we fire to the top. Our numbers were out of control, we couldn't keep up with business, and the money was fantastic. I was living a life that I really didn't think would be possible: Fancy cars, beautiful dinners, amazing holidays and the bank account was full. But, it still wasn't enough.

I was promoted to a national role and travel became an everyday thing. I was losing friends, I was not enjoying the fake picture of success I had painted for everybody to see, and the worst of it all was that my relationship with

Mel began to suffer. I became very depressed and would cry daily about the life that I had created. I had painted the perfect picture of success.

We had the sports cars, the fancy apartment and the big bank account, but I had an empty heart. I was missing my partner, missing my family and some days I just didn't really want to get out of bed. I realised that I could keep pushing up the corporate ladder, make more money, and buy nicer things, but probably end-up broken and alone.

I realised my priorities, and that was my family, so we both decided to move back to Coffs Harbour to be closer to them. I was offered the Bank Manager job for Westpac, and I thought that this could really assist us with stability and allow us to start fresh, close to our old friends.

Things started very well for both of us. Mel had a steady job and I was enjoying my wonderful new team in Coffs Harbour. One day, I decided to make the ultimate commitment by asking for Mel's hand in marriage.

It was the hardest conversation I had ever had at that point in my life when I asked her father, Steve, whether I could marry his beautiful daughter. Steve and I bumped heads a lot, unfortunately. I just wanted him to like me, but I think that we may have been so similar in terms of our desire to succeed in the corporate world, so we clashed a little, which made the question even harder, although we have since become great friends.

I finally built-up the courage to ask as I was racing to the airport, which was not the greatest of places to ask and if I had my time over, I would have really made more effort, because I truly loved his daughter more then anything in the world. I got his approval and we flew to Bali on a little getaway.

I had only picked up the ring on my way to the airport after locking it away in my mum's cupboard for safe keeping and so no snoopers i.e. Mel would find it. We arrived at the airport and I realised that I still had the ring box in the top pocket of my jeans and thought that if I went through security with her and had to take it out, she will see it and the surprise would have been over. Panicking, I sent her in before me to start checking in and managed to open up the luggage and sneak it into a pair of socks.

I had hired a restaurant in the hills of Ubud, and there were candles and rose petals everywhere: "You are my life; Will you be my wife?", which I asked just as a cover artist started singing all of Mel's favourite Michael Bublé songs. I got down on one knee and asked her to make me the happiest man on the planet. She said yes.

We came home from our holiday and celebrated with all our family and friends. We had two amazing engagement parties: One here in Coffs Harbour with our wonderful friends and family, and then another gathering in Sydney.

But then it was back to work. Westpac gave me an opportunity to stretch, and again, I was burning the candle at both ends. I had five sites to juggle, and the ongoing roles of keeping my staff, my family and my Mel happy.

I felt as though I was failing in all departments. The dark thoughts of depression kicked back in, and I was not enjoying life. From the outside in, I looked as though I had it made. I had a beautiful, soon to be wife, lovely home, great car, awesome job, and I was surrounded by great people. But inside, I was alone; I was lost and I was stressed.

I think that stress is something that is crippling and debilitating. It's something that can suck you down and hold on to you for as long as you let it. People say that positive thinking can help reduce stress and sometimes dissolve it all together. My opinion is that positive thinking doesn't mean that you keep your head in the sand and ignore life's less pleasant situations. Positive thinking just means that you approach unpleasantness in a more positive and productive way.

You think the best is going to happen, not the worst. Positive thinking often starts with self-talk, which is the endless stream of unspoken thoughts that run through your head. These automatic thoughts can be positive or negative.

Some of your self-talk comes from logic and reason. Other self-talk may arise from misconceptions that you create because of lack of information. If the thoughts that run through your head are mostly negative, your outlook on life is more likely to be pessimistic.

If your thoughts are mostly positive, you're likely an optimist. But at this point in my life, I was only looking at the glass that was half empty, not the glass that was half full. I was Mr Pessimistic, and I had lost clarity, direction and purpose.

But why after all that I had been through? I think it was that I had worked so hard to reach a certain level in the corporate field, which I thought was going to bring me joy and happiness, but it only brought me money and stress.

One afternoon when I was at the office, I started to feel horrible and my head started to pound; my neck was sore, my eyes were aching, and then I realised I was drooling out the side of my mouth.

My PA came in and said: "What has happened to your face?" It had dropped down on the right side. I was taken to hospital and was informed that I had Bell's Palsy, which is almost like a stroke that affected me on my right side. I was a little lost soul. I would not talk to anyone, I didn't want visitors, and when my wife would leave the room of a night time, I would pray.

It was not the same prayer that I said when I was a child who wanted to go home and get out of the hospital; it was something much darker than that. It hurts me to think that I was ever in a place to pray for this, but I did. Each night, I would pray to God that I would not wake up in the morning.

I didn't want to face the challenges anymore, I didn't want to be sick or stressed; I just wanted to rest and be at peace. But God never listened and I kept waking up each morning and, day by day, I got stronger and stronger, not only physically, but more importantly, mentally.

CHAPTER TEN

LIVING INTO MY LEGACY

"I reflect and think life is so short; if you're not loving who you are
and what you're doing, then make the change to become your best."
Michael Crossland

When I got out of hospital, I made the bold decision to walk away from the corporate life and to follow my dream of making a global impact as an inspirational speaker, sharing my thoughts, ideas and stories with the world. People laughed, and others told me that I was crazy to walk away from a wonderful career to follow something that sounded so unsubstantial and wistful. Yet, I think in life that is part of the fun: simply not knowing what is around the corner.

I needed to master a few things in life: I needed to master the gift of giving. I needed to truly understand what success was, and I needed to begin to live into my legacy.

I had the support of my fiancé to walk away from a very healthy salary to follow a goal and a vision, where our futures were completely uncertain, and with no idea at all as to where it would lead us today.

Still, I thought I needed to give back in areas where I thought I could make a difference. The answer was staring right at me in the face. There was a picture of me with some friends at Camp Quality as a child. I thought: "I am going to become a companion and spend time with these little angels who are coping with so much and dealing with something that I completely understand."

Camp Quality gave me so much for so long, and now I was finally in a position to give back, I had plenty of time and I took my wife along with me to Camp Quality and we both become companions.

On my first camp, a little boy came up to me and gave me a big hug. He had been very unwell. His name was Christian, and I remember the day that I met this little guy, I knew that he was going to be a part of my life forever. He brought such happiness into my life.

I reflect back on my own experiences as a child with my own Camp Quality Companion, and I hope that this was the same happiness that I brought into my companion, Simon's life, back in the 1980s.

Damien Ford Photography ©

I was inspired by Christian's courage, optimism, and his smiles. I reflect on so many things throughout my life when somebody has given to me, and it's made me feel good, but when I have given to them or given to someone else, the feeling is so much greater. I think that the saying: "You receive far more from giving than you'll ever receive from receiving" is so true.

The happiness and the joy that it brings to you when making a difference to others is so much better than when somebody makes a difference to you. We had so many fun times on camp.

Christian was the camp prankster; he loved to prank anybody and everybody all the time. I remember on my first camp, he was going around putting little cups of flour on the tops of all of the doors, so that when people walked into the room, they would open the door and a cup of flour would fall on them.

I remember he laced the top of my fan in my room one day with powder so that when it got really hot, I would turn the fan on and flour would go everywhere in the room. Somehow, he managed to catch a wild turkey and stick the turkey on top of my bed, and when I came into the room at night, there was a crazy turkey sitting on my bed.

He filled up my sleeping bag with Weet-Bix and corn flakes, and I remember one day he put cling wrap over the toilet, so when I raced to the toilet, I wasn't going into the toilet. To hear his laughter and to hear the joy in his voice, to see him be a normal kid and just have fun, demonstrates so powerfully and so beautifully the impact that Camp Quality has on so many different people.

Today, I'm still Christian's companion, but he's much more than that; he is my friend and always will be. He's healthy and he's happy and it's so wonderful to be a part of his journey.

In 2012, I became the National Ambassador for Camp Quality, which makes me a large part of so many different fundraising events around the country.

I'm very proud to say, my contribution has resulted in over $1,000,000 that has been raised for this great charity. I believe it costs $880 to send a child to Camp Quality each year, so I think about the $1,000,000+ raised, and I realise that it is a lot of kids who are getting a great opportunity to be a part of something so special.

Camp Quality also helped me so much to break into the speaking world, and they also helped to open the door for me to be a part of the Canterbury-Bankstown Bulldogs.

I think to really make it in the speaking world you need a thick skin and a relentless determination to simply be able to break down the barriers and get on stage to share your message. But there's always that underlying importance of being at the right place at the right time.

One day, I received a phone call from the CEO of Camp Quality, Simon Rowntree. He said: "Michael, we're wondering whether you would be available to share your journey with the Canterbury Bulldogs NRL team?" I was so excited and could not wait to seize this opportunity as I love rugby league, even though I did not know much about the Bulldogs or their players.

I made sure that I was available and got on the plane to speak to the team. I called a friend of mine, Simon O'Dell, who came along to film the presentation, as this was a massive step into the professional sporting world.

We arrived at the auditorium and set up. I remember Des Hasler, the head coach, walked in and said: "Michael are you ready to go, you all good, you need anything, you're ready, is it all good?" He was an intense character who spoke very fast, but he was extremely passionate about this game, so I was pumped and ready!

When everybody arrived, I realised that there were no players in attendance; it was only front office staff, management, board members and coaching staff. I've got to be honest and say that I was a little bit disappointed, but it was still a great opportunity to be a part of a very successful sporting team.

The presentation went very well. In fact, it went so well that Des and the CEO, Todd Greenburg, invited me back the following week to speak to all of the players. I remember sending a photo to my cousin, who has been a Bulldogs fan all his life, asking him whether he could tell me the names of the people who were in the photo with me; I had no idea who they were!

You can imagine that his response was rather explicit, because he would've done anything to be in that room with those players. The Bulldogs invited me to all of their home games, and I became very close friends with many of the players. I am not sure whether it was coincidence or luck, but from then on, they went on to achieve a 12 game winning streak and they made the grand final. I had to do the right thing by my cousin, Nathan, so I took him to the grand final game; otherwise he probably would have never forgiven me.

Unfortunately, they were beaten, but what a wonderful experience to be a part of that journey. I still continue to interact with this club and their players to this day. To be in and around the club during the transformation that the club has had over the last four or five years has been phenomenal.

Again, being able to get involved with the Bulldogs opened me up to building relationships with players, and I now maintain such strong relationships and bonds with Trent Hodkinson, Josh Reynolds, Josh Morris, and Mick Ennis. Mick Ennis is a real blessing, and it all come off the back of this amazing organization, called Camp Quality. Still, as you know, my passion has always been Baseball, and to be able to speak to baseball players and professional athletes would be a real dream come true.

I was speaking to all of the athletes at a college in America when a gentleman said to me: "Michael, I'm going to arrange for you to speak to the Toronto Bluejays." If I had a dollar for every time someone had offered me to speak somewhere, life would be very different. Unfortunately, many people will offer you the world and deliver you absolutely nothing.

This has happened to me over and over again. I get that on a regular basis because I get caught up in the excitement of other people's ideas and connections, which sadly, often lead nowhere! So, I thanked him for his kind offer and thought to myself: "Yup; just another offer that will go nowhere." Nevertheless, this guy's name was Steve Springer, and to be honest, I had no idea who he was.

But he was a man of his word, and he was going to make this happen. After doing a little research, I realised that he had played in the big leagues and he was now the hitting coach for some of the best hitters in the MLB.

I can't tell you the sheer excitement that ran through my veins, nor the exhilaration and pride of my family, when I received an email from the Bluejays asking for my availability during their Spring Training camp in March. I realised that this was really going to happen: Mixing my love of baseball with my career as a speaker.

The flight was long and flying economy class was a little uncomfortable, yet those things were put aside and overtaken by the sheer excitement of getting a chance to spend time with some of the best baseball players on the planet. Arriving at Spring Training camp, seeing the freshly cut grass, the perfectly aligned field, and seeing the amazing stadium, was indescribable.

I had goosebumps, and it was almost like something I had worked so hard for and for so long had finally come true. Meeting the coaching staff, front office employees and then the players: What an experience that was, and then as if that was not enough, I had the opportunity to share my journey with them on stage.

I also had the chance to throw at batting practice, and spend time on the field. I also got to go out for dinner with them, which was a real treat and a memory that I will treasure for a lifetime. It's awesome years later that I still have these people in my life, and I still have the opportunity to go back to Spring Training every year .

In 2015 I had a very special trip to Spring Training, because I spent time with one of my sporting idols whose turn double plays I used to watch when I was in hospital in Sydney; My Mum always tried to tape the games that he played in.

His name was Roberto Alomar. The day he came to Spring Training, drove me around in his Bentley, and went out to lunch with me, was certainly a highlight of my life. The Bluejays made it all the way through the play-offs and just missed out on playing in the World Series; what an amazing experience to have been a part of that ride!

One day, I was asked to speak at a conference in Denver, Colorado. It was going to open many doors and give me great exposure in the American market (which I later realised was not the case), and they said: "We have no budget, but we really want these kids to hear your story."

So I decided to make the journey to the other side of the world to share my story with these underprivileged college students, but what I didn't realise was that this was going to change my outlook on life forever.

After a very long trip, I finally arrived in Denver, went to the hotel, checked in, had a quick shower, and went downstairs to share my story with the audience. It was the longest Q&A session post presentation that I have ever had. These kids were so engaged. I was so present; they were like sponges and just wanted to learn and soak up everything I had to give them.

I found out whilst I was there that the total combined income for parents of these students attending this event could not be more than $20,000 a year. These were kids that are faced some pretty nasty challenges, and it really became an honour to make an impact on these kids' lives.

After I left Denver, it was a long flight back to Australia, and three weeks went by during which time I continually thought about these amazing people that were just so passionate about life, and one day, I received a letter in the mail.

The letter began with the caption: "I use the rope to play tug-of-war." It was a letter from a young lady who was sitting in the front row, whom I recalled very clearly. She was quite a large young lady, she was wearing lots of black make-up, black nail varnish, her dress was black, and she painted a picture of what many people categorise as Gothic.

The letter went on to tell me that she had been raped by her father, and when she told her mother she was bashed repeatedly, because the mother thought that she was lying and was trying to cause drama within the family.

She really didn't fit in at her college, she didn't have many friends, and she really just didn't connect well with the world. The morning of my presentation, she went to the local hardware store and bought a long piece of rope and tied it up in her hotel room inside the cupboard.

There was a knock on her door, and it was one of the teachers informing her that she must come down to hear a guy from Australia speak, but she told the teacher that she was not feeling well and that she was going to stay in her room.

She was going to do the unthinkable. The teacher persisted and insisted that she go downstairs to hear the Australian man speak, because he had flown a long way to be there, so everyone needed to attend. So as frustrated and angry as she was, she went downstairs to listen to my speech.

In her letter to me, she said that something changed in her mind about ending her life prematurely; she had gotten greater clarity around her purpose, and she went on to tell me that she realised her adversity, her pain, and her challenges in life did not need to define her, but could instead give her strength to appreciate the finer things in life.

So, rather than going back to her room to kill herself after my talk, she decided to untie the rope, and head downstairs to play tug-of-war with all the other kids. Because she was a large girl, everybody wanted her on their team; she became the anchor and they won every challenge.

She said that date had changed her life. The other kids realised that she was a lovely girl, and just because she dressed differently, it didn't make her a bad person.

I reflect on this letter regularly and I think to myself how lucky I am to be in the position I am: By simply sharing my adversities, my challenges, and my stories, I can have a positive impact on others, and I may even save someone's life.

I wanted people to understand that it's not materialistic possessions and money that change people; it can be something as simple as a smile. Smiling is one of the special abilities that is associated with being human.

It is the best way to express a great mood, and it is a powerful way to share these happy feelings with others. Smiling also functions as a symbol to express love, friendship, and care; it is recognised by others as something that comes from your heart. Some people say that smiling is transmittable or contagious, because no-one wants to live in an unhappy world; they prefer to spend their time around those people who always wear a smile on their face and with people who can enjoy a great laugh.

There is a saying that smiling makes you live longer, because it it will lead us to healthier and a happier living. We can attain more health benefits in smiling, too. Most of the doctors who treated me said that laughter is the best medicine, just like Camp Quality's motto.

For me, a smile also reduces stress and makes me much more relaxed. Giving the sweetest smile to someone will ease his or her problems and loneliness and will cost you absolutely nothing. I think that it also strengthens our immune system, which is certainly something very important for me.

A smile is the ambassador of your goodwill. It brightens up the life of those people who see someone smiling at them. It is like a sunrise that gives light

to darkest of days. I often like to pose the following question to people: "What am I? I cost nothing, but I create much. I enrich those who receive me, without impoverishing those who give me.

I happen in a flash, but their memory of me sometimes lasts a lifetime." Your smile can be a game changer.

In April, 2012, after several trips to the States speaking, we finally had enough money to get married. It was such a special day at the beautiful Bonville Golf Resort among wonderful family and friends. Later that year, we went on our honeymoon to Fiji for seven nights.

Unfortunately, I spent six of the seven nights in bed sick. I became very unwell after a big speaking tour and my body was exhausted. Still, I was not alone; I had my beautiful wife playing nurse and looking after me.

She would sun-bake on the balcony, and I would rest up in the shade. It really hit me throughout our honeymoon just how lucky I am to have this amazing wife a part of my life forever.

We then traveled to the States for two weeks to spend time with friends who now feel like family.

It was a really wonderful trip, and it allowed us to truly be together and to be truly present with each other.

CHAPTER ELEVEN

POWER OF GIVING

"Climb the mountain so you can see the world,
not so the world can see you." David McCullough

"A life of giving is a life worth living." Rob Elings

"Master the gift of giving and you will
master the gift of life." Michael Crossland

"Our days are happier when we give people a bit of our heart
rather than a piece of our mind." Unknown

"Small acts of kindness, when multiplied by millions,
can truly transform this world" Howard Zinn

"Do something helpful/kind/nice for someone else,
expecting nothing in return." Michael Crossland

When we returned home from our honeymoon, we bought ourselves a nice home in sunny Sawtell. We loved the location, because it is close to beaches, and our family and friends. The house was no mansion; it was a modest home and was all that we required. It was on a nice large block with four bedrooms and we loved the backyard.

One day, Mel asked me whether we could get a fireplace. I've always been taught that a good husband says the two words that we must understand clearly, and those two words are: "Yes, dear." So needless to say, we got the fireplace. But I am not handy. In fact, I'm probably on the other end of the spectrum of "handy"; I am hopeless when it comes to either building or fixing things.

We hired a friend to come around to install the fireplace. He eventually got to the point where he was putting in the down pipe, and he asked me whether I could give him a hand. I, of course, jumped to his aid, and I said: What can I do?

He asked me whether I could just catch the stainless steel pipe and put it into place as he lowered it from the roof. Unfortunately, when he was reaching down from the roof, he dropped it and it severed the tendons, nerves and ligaments in my thumb! Blood went everywhere and made an absolute mess. He drove me straight to the hospital, and fortunately enough, I am pretty well-known at the hospital, because I've spent a lot of time there. I went straight into surgery.

Whilst waiting to go in, I noticed a little boy with a big smile on his face lying next to me in another bed. I thought that this was quite strange as everybody in this room was going into surgery. I guess the morphine drugs had really kicked in. A nurse walked in and pulled the sheets back to see what his issue was, and she said: "Oh, my God! What has happened to you?"

The little boy went on to tell the nurse what had happened. He said that he had been riding his quad bike through the bush, he had fallen off it, and a stick had lodged itself into his leg. Yet, he finished the sentence with something that I thought was pretty powerful. He finished by saying: "But nurse, it could be worse."

The nurse immediately questioned his logic and queried how it could possibly be worse: "You have a stick in your leg, you aren't going to be able to go swimming, you will be on crutches, you will have to have surgery; what do you mean it could be worse?"

Still, the little boy with the big smile on his face insisted to the nurse that it could have been worse: "The stick could have got me in the balls." I roared laughing and so did everybody else in the room, including the nurse. I can just imagine the father saying to the little boy on the way to the hospital: "Son, quit your whinging; the stick could've got you in the balls!", and immediately, he would have stopped crying.

Not only is this a very funny story, but I feel that this story is so much deeper than is originally apparent. I think that what this little boy said is something so true, and his message is something for us all to live our lives by. Regardless of our adversities, our pain, and our suffering, it could always be worse, and it's not our adversity that defines us, but rather, it's all about how we deal with it.

All we need to do these days is to switch on the TV to see how much hatred and pain is in the world. From people killing others at pubs, kids bullying other kids, divorce rates skyrocketing, to the horrible and heartbreaking terrorist attacks that are destroying entire communities and countries forever, it is so clear that our own adversities could be far worse. We need to appreciate each day and learn to not only love one another, but to also give back to the world.

I started to realise that I could not settle for just travelling, speaking, sharing, and using the power of a smile with anybody and everybody; I needed something more. I needed to master the power and the gift of giving. I needed others to realise that, regardless of whether you're the rich guy or the poor guy, we all have the same opportunity to give, whether it's helping an old lady across the road, helping someone to unpack their trolley full of groceries, or giving someone a smile. Something as simple as sharing a smile with somebody can really change someone's life. For me, that is how I really needed to live my life.

Through the challenges that I continue to face, mastering the gift of giving was going to shape my future. Because for me, when I worked in the corporate world, I was very driven by the three P's: The Power, the Privileges, and the Possessions, and even though I gained all of those, I wasn't happy. I wasn't enjoying life. And the one thing that I didn't focus on was happiness. When you start to shape your outlook on life purely around happiness, it's amazing what you can achieve.

I guess in life your dreams are one thing, but the reason behind those dreams is something far greater. The joy of accomplishing something is amazing. When you realize that you can help other people achieve similar dreams, it far outweighs the joy that you receive when you achieved your own.

I continued to participate in the Aussie Expos Baseball program that had taken me to the States many times over in the past, and I became a member of the coaching staff.

Unfortunately, my dear friend, mentor and former coach, John Murray, passed away after years of sickness. The program was no longer going to continue.

That same year that the program was meant to cease, I made a promise to a little boy by the name of Sean Richards; Sean Richards was a perfect stranger, but he was to later become a very important part of my family. He, unfortunately, had a very bad go-kart accident just before Christmas and was given two bits of news. The good news was he didn't have a broken back.

The bad news was they had found a tumour in his spine, and it didn't look good. I made a commitment to him to stay strong and to keep close to his side throughout his cancer battle. I promised him that I would take him to America, because like me, it was his dream to one day play baseball in America.

Obviously, the program couldn't finish when I'd made that commitment. I asked the Murray family whether they would allow me to continue the program in honor of the legacy that their father had left. They agreed, and I was fortunate to be able to take this little boy to America to live his dreams. Just like me when I played over there as a child, he was definitely not the biggest or the fastest.

He was, in fact, the smallest and probably the slowest, but we wanted to make sure his dream came true.

I remember putting him out onto the field. It was the last inning of this game. We were winning by two runs. We put him at second base, and all of a sudden, the American team started to swing the bat. Base hit here. Base hit there. Stolen base here. Extra base hit there. It was a three-two ballgame, with one out and loaded bases.

The young American boy stepped up to the plate and hit the ball hard into the gap between shortstop and third. The shortstop backhanded the ball and fired it over to Sean, who just happened to be standing on second base. We were hoping that the ball didn't hit him, but it managed to hit him all right; right in the middle of the glove. He caught the ball, and then to our immense joy and excitement, he stepped on second base .

We immediately thought: "That's fabulous. Now they've scored a run and its a three all ball game, but there's two out. Hopefully, we can get the last out and go in the extra innings." However, *Sean* had a different outcome in his mind. He stepped off second base.

He fired the ball to first, and he turned the game ending into winning

double play. Talk about tears of joy and tears of happiness! That was a moment in my life that I will never forget; it was a moment where I realised that I had just helped somebody else's dream come true, and it would change their life forever.

Now, I've been a part of that program and continue to be a part of that program as the tour manager and director. I hope to continue the legacy that John Murray has left by helping others to live out their dream of playing baseball in America.

Two years ago, I was fortunate to take a boy by the name of Todd Nester. He was a contestant on the award-winning Australian TV show, The Biggest Loser. He had lost 38 kilos in less than four months. I found out via that programme that his dream was also to play baseball in America. It was a real treat to be able to take him over there and allow him to be a part of that program.

In summary of my baseball journey, it started off as a dream for me about what I could do as an athlete, and what I could do as a baseball player. Now, it's turned into something far greater than that. It's become a job where I can help, educate, hone skills, teach other people, and give other people the opportunity to live their dreams. For me, that is just a great joy and a great gift, which I'm lucky to share with so many people around the world now.

But that's not where the beginning stopped; instead, it was where the beginning started.

On January 12, 2010, an earthquake hit Haiti, Port-au- Prince. It killed approximately 316,000 people, and it left millions of people homeless. Haiti is around one third of the size of Tasmania. Yet, it has a population of over 10 million people.

The devastation was absolutely abhorrent, and it made worldwide news. A significant amount of money was donated to Haiti to try to rescue them from the devastation. Unfortunately, a massive amount of corruption saw a lot of that money disappear. The support and the aid just never arrived.

In 2012, I was fortunate to venture down to Haiti with some dear friends, Cheryl and John Ward, who have become lifelong friends. When you experience something so graphic and as heartbreaking as being in that environment, it changes you forever.

Your outlook, your perspective, your thoughts on humankind, definitely change.

You begin to ask a lot of questions: "Why?" "Why is the world the way that it is?" "Why does devastation have to debilitate, not only families, but communities, towns, and an entire nation?"

I reflect back on my first time visiting Haiti. I flew from Coffs Harbour, the beautiful coastal town of Northern New South Wales, and I landed in the busy city of Sydney. I flew from Sydney to L.A., where there are millions and millions of people, and where there is wealth. I flew from L.A. to Miami, where wealth goes to an extreme level.

There are houses that are valued in the vicinity of 15 to 20 million dollars, which are sitting on the edge of pristine waterways. Then, I boarded a plane, by myself, with 165 other people, 165 of whom were Haitians. I was the only white guy who got on the plane.

I landed in Port-au-Prince to be greeted by the smell of death, decaying bodies, sewage, the heat, the humidity, and the noise of people yelling and screaming as they saw me arrive, and try to grab me through the fence. I went through customs, and the man stared at me. He didn't say a word, but slammed the stamp down on my passport, and looked up, as if to say: "Off you go."

I arrived inside a little tin shed, where they throw your bags from the carousel onto the ground in a massive mound. People just dived in and grabbed their bags. I got my bag, and there were people with red shirts everywhere, trying to carry my bag out, so I gave them money. I just carried my own bag and I started walking out, knowing that there would be a man in a car, waiting for me to go.

I walked down a very narrow corridor, with a tin roof cover over the top, which was now outside. There was a barbed wire fence, either side of me. I heard people yelling in Creole; they were spitting and trying to grab me as I walked right down the middle, so I felt a little safe.

I waited for 15 minutes; the traffic was horrendous, so my lift was late. I got into the car. The broken windows were replaced with plastic bags. The smell of burning rubber and burning plastic just filled the air. We drive for miles and miles, and the depth of the devastation started to kick in.

My emotions took over, and you could not help but cry. I saw people who were completely and utterly helpless. They had nothing: No families, no roof over their heads. No drinking water.

No place to even go to the bathroom. I could see people begging on the side of the street, their hands and their feet missing, with just bandages around them. I saw young women, young boys and girls, urinating in the street, because there was nowhere else to go.

Every time we would stop at traffic lights, there would be people knocking on the window, begging for money. The smell was something that I can't possibly explain in words. Your breath shortens, so as to minimise the horrific smell that consumes your nasal passages, your throat, and into your lungs. The traffic was worse than what you would see in downtown L.A.

We were literally stationary for 15, 20, 25 and 30 minutes at a time, without the wheels rolling an inch. Every now and then, the car would get stuck where there was someone burning their plastic. The smell of plastic just wafted through, and I needed to wrap my face up with a jumper to try to take away the smell, so I could hardly breathe.

We arrived at a little shop, where were going to get some food before we trekked up the mountain, because that is why we were there. We found out that many of these children were walking four or five hours a day, simply to try to get to school. Some of the things that were happening to them, not only on their way to school, but on their way home, were just horrific.

We felt that this was the place where we could add value. This was a place where we could go along to rebuild something very important, like education. We'd try to break the mould, or break the cycle, and allow these people to get on their feet, so they could start to realise that they had a future. There is always hope, and there are people who genuinely care.

We walked into a shop, and as we were walking out, a nine year old boy ran past us carrying a loaf of bread; he got shot by the security guard, because he was trying to steal bread for his starving family.

You reflect on days when you complained about how bad the traffic was, how uncomfortable your bed is sometimes, how hot you are, how cold your are, how you don't want to do an assignment, how you don't want to dial into that conference call, and how you don't really want to go to work today. You quickly realise, with a grinding shock, that your First World problems pale into insignificance compared with what these people face and experience every single day.

We drove for two hours to get us to the base of where we started to trek. We went past crushed buildings, where there were just little crosses out the front of where the buildings had been. We found out that many of the bodies were still inside, because they don't have the infrastructure to get them out. We began to trek up the mountain.

I finally met my Australian friends. The trek takes about ten hours, and I knew that it was going to be a great challenge, because it was a very steep walk. We had to carry a lot of tools for the build. We got about an hour into the trek, and I said to one of the guys who was directing us: "How far to go?" He replied: "We're halfway." I thought: "Fantastic, we've only got an hour to go."

Then, what felt like another three hours went by, and I asked him, "How far are we?" He said, "Halfway." Three hours later, I noted that we were four hours into the journey, and it was only then that we were halfway.

Water supply was about a third gone. We got about six hours into the trek, and I asked the man: "How far are we away?" He responded: "We're halfway." Now, I started to panic, because we had been trekking for six hours. He had told me that we were halfway, so my immediate thought was that we still had another six hours to go. I looked down, and my bottle of water was empty.

The temperature was around 42 degrees Celsius and 110 degrees Fahrenheit. I was very dehydrated. My knees started to ache. My ankles were sore. My heart was beating out of my chest, and all I could think of was having a cold drink.

We got to the base of the last climb, and there was a fresh water stream. Unfortunately, it was not fresh enough to drink, but it was certainly fresh enough to swim in. It reduced my body temperature and made me feel so much better. All the pain seemed to go away as my body temperature reduced.

When I got out of the water, they gave me a tin can of tomato juice, because that was the only liquid that we had left. I cracked open the tin of tomato juice. I had half a mouthful, and then I begin to vomit violently and profusely .

It was something that my body definitely did not need. I realised that all I needed to do was to get to the site where we were building the school, so I would be able to get some fresh water. We were another hour in, so the trek had now gone for seven, nearly eight hours.

I asked my buddy, "How far are we in?" He answered: "We're halfway." I realised, then and there, that's about all he could say in English: "We're halfway."

Finally, we stopped at a tiny little campsite, and there was a lady who had a familiar face. I was absolutely delighted, because she was there with a bottle of clean water. I wanted to drink it all, but I realised that there were many of us, and we were all very dehydrated. We passed the water around, and we only had one hour of climbing to go.

We were about 20 minutes into that last hour, and my body just seemed to begin to fail. There were seven little girls, all carrying very heavy bottles of water on their head. It was almost like there were seven little angels who just wouldn't leave me. I sat under a tree, because I needed to get some energy back, and so did they. I didn't want to get up, but they helped me up.

When the trek become narrow, they would stand behind me to help me up the hills. These beautiful little kids had just walked four hours down and four hours back to get some fresh water out of the pond, so that they had water they could drink.

However, they needed to take it back to the house to boil it to try to kill all the germs. They walked beside me. They walked behind me. They walked with me all the way, until we got to the site where we were going to build the school. Then, they continued on into their village.

We got to a flat area, where the concrete had already been laid, and the view was breath-taking. This is where the site was for us to rebuild the school. Over the next two weeks, we battled every day, all day and all night. During the day, the temperatures got up to as high as 44 degrees Celsius, and of a night, it would get as low as five or six degrees.

It was a fascinating climate, because we would need to get changed into our bed clothes by 6:00pm. Otherwise, it would get so cold, that you would feel like you were going to catch pneumonia, even though, just a couple hours earlier, you would be so hot, you would just constantly sweat.

Two weeks went by, and we managed to build something that was so special. These kids no longer had to walk hours and hours of a day and a night to get an education. The school had come to them. The saying: "If you build it, they will come", was so true. Within the first week of opening this school, there were 120 kids attending the school. Within one year, we have 230 children going to this school every single day.

We have five, full-time teachers, and a principal who lives onsite to support these kids. To see the impact of giving to other people is one of the greatest feelings of all.

I went to Haiti, because I wanted to make a difference in other people's lives. At the same time, I thought to myself: "If I can go over there and help them, it'll be one of those feelings where I've been able to help somebody, but they can never repay me."

I was so mistaken, because the joy that they brought into my life far outweighs the joy that I've brought into theirs. My time in Haiti had only just begun, because my life changed forever when I trekked back from that mountain.

We arrived at an orphanage. There were 20 little kids. They had no clothes, no food, and no shelter, but they all had one thing in common: Astoundingly, they all had a smile on their face. These kids had nothing. They had no mum or dad.

They had lost everything in the earthquake. Yet, they still had life. They still had dreams. They still had hope for a brighter future.

It was something that has helped me become the person I am today, because it put so many things into perspective. I asked the little boy the best part about being here, and he commented that he gets a bowl of rice every other day. The worst part is the fact that he has to share a bed with two little boys who both still pee their pants, and they all get soaking wet at night.

In my life, I spend so much time on the roads and in hotels. Sometimes I complain about the hotels where I am staying. I walk into the room, I see ten pillows on the bed, and I think to myself: "What do I need with 10 pillows? I only need one." After I remove nine pillows, I go to climb into bed, and I think that the cleaner must think that I am a cardboard cut-out; they tuck the sheets in so flipping tight that you need to rip out the sheets just so you can get into the bed. Then, your feet are so squashed at the end of the bed that they feel like flippers.

How dare I complain: These guys are not complaining because the roof leaks, because they have no family, and the little boy is not complaining because he is getting peed on. These kids are celebrating each day the mere fact that they are alive; they are breathing. They count their blessings every day, not their problems.

The happiest people don't have the best of everything; they just make the best of everything. I think to myself throughout these hard times and challenging moments: "A star does not shine without darkness". These angels are certainly shining in my heart.

The plight of the people of Haiti tore out my heart, and I really felt I needed to do something. My friends and I went back to Australia, and we raised a whole heap of money. Then, a dear friend of mine, Simon O'Dell, and I got on a plane and ventured back to Haiti together in order to rebuild the orphanage from the ground up. I remember the first day I was there. We were exhausted.

We were lying in a tiny concrete shack, and the heat was overwhelming: the noise, the smell, the mosquitoes, the uncomfortable bed, with just a tiny fan on the end of my bed to keep me cool. There was a noise of a generator outside, constantly murmuring, making a horrible racket. I got next to no sleep, and I had to film the very next morning.

I remember waking up and saying to the man who was running that area: "Why, why, did you need that generator going all night? The bed was uncomfortable. The mosquitoes were biting me. The noise was horrendous. The temperature was brutal." I recall he said to me: "Michael, I'm sorry I can't do anything about the heat. Nor can I do anything about the comfort of your bed, or the mosquitoes." He added: "And I'm sorry about the noise from the generator, but I had one of the young orphans sleep on the roof, where the generator sits, and he topped up the generator with fuel, every two hours, to make sure that we had enough power to run the fan on the end of your bed."

Sometimes it's so powerful when you step out of your own shoes and look at life through someone else's eyes. You quickly begin to realise that your problems, your challenges, your adversity, your pain, and your suffering can be so insignificant in comparison to the struggles of people who live in the Third World.

The next two weeks were the hardest and the most emotionally draining, but they were the most rewarding experience of my life. There was not one day on the work site where we felt alone.

There was not one day where there wasn't a seven-year-old boy, with no mum or dad or brothers or sisters, without a hammer in his hand, and a nail, ready to do whatever it took to help these people.

I remember that one day Simon and I went down to buy the beds—the new beds that these kids were going to sleep in. So many of them were just lying on pieces of tin, or timber, or steel. The first shop we went into, we found that the mattresses were $100 each. When Simon and I walked into pay, they quickly increased that amount to $380 per mattress.

We had only been funded $2,000 for 20 mattresses. There was no way in the world that we were going to be able to afford it. What we had to do was go to other stores, stay on the back of the truck, and let the guys from the orphanage go in to pay for it to prevent us from being ripped off.

We had a security guard, Samuel, who stayed on the edge of the truck with us the whole time. After purchasing the mattresses, he left the truck to go in to get the mattresses. Talk about fear and anxiety!

We were in this scary place, where people wanted a piece of us, because we weren't helping them. The truck started to be surrounded by people, and not nice people; they were people who had machetes, and people who wanted our money.

They were people who wanted us to help them, not help the people we were helping. Fortunately enough, our prayers were answered: When Samuel and the rest of the team came running out with mattresses, they all ran off, so we were okay.

We went back to the orphanage with all of our gear, and we transformed the orphanage from a run-down, old tin shack to somewhere that these kids could call home. We turned it into something that these kids were proud of. They helped paint the walls. They helped put the beds together. They helped create something that was special to them.

There's been plenty of memories of my time in Haiti. Good memories, bad memories, sad and emotional memories, but I continue to reflect on why I went there in the first place. I went there because I wanted to make a difference in someone's life, where they could never, ever make a difference in mine. Surprise! They made more of a difference in mine than I could ever make in theirs.

Nine months later, I was fortunate to get on the plane to head back over there with a very dear friend of mine, Wayne Glenn, a member of the Coffs Harbour Rotary Team. Very sadly, Wayne passed away only recently.

We went over there to put a second storey on the orphanage, and to put new beds and more mattresses in there. We also built them a kitchen, a toilet, and a shower. When they first saw the toilet, these kids had no idea what to do. They thought it was a basin to drink out of. It really smacks you in the face when you need to educate a 10-year- old boy on how to use a toilet, because they've never seen one before.

These people, have a heart for giving. These people would give you the last dime they had. They would give you the last piece of food they had. They would take the clothes off their back for you, to provide for you.

It's interesting to see so many videos nowadays online, where a homeless man will go up and ask a very wealthy man who is eating a pizza whether he can have a piece, and the wealthy man replies: "No."

They will ask a wealthy lady who gets change from her purchase at Myers whether they could borrow a dollar, and she'll reply: "No." Then, they set up a scene where they have a homeless man who is given a pizza, and another man will walk past and ask: "Is there any chance I could have a piece of pizza?", and the homeless man quickly gives him half of his pizza.

Why is it that the more we gain in life, the more we expect? But, when we lose everything, it's almost like our outlook completely changes, and we realise that giving is so much more powerful and so much more rewarding than receiving?

CHAPTER TWELVE

TOOLS TO SHIFT YOUR MINDSET

"When you change the way you look at things,
the things you look at change" Wayne Dyer

"I believe the major cause of unhappiness is never the situation
but your thoughts about the situation! Embrace the challenge,
empower the mind and smile." Michael Crossland

Many people ask me how I manage to stay so positive and upbeat through some of the dark days. I use a very simple, yet effective tool; its all about living above the line. It's the difference between being a Victim or a Navigator.

This principle is all about the line of life. This line can apply to your business, your personal life, your relationships, your challenges, and your adversities. This principle is something you can use in every single part of your life. I promise you that all the people you look up to in the world, whether they are a public figure or not, live this principle that I am about to share.

If it is the only thing that you take away from this book, you will become a better human being if you can grasp this and apply it each day with your husband, wife, partner, children, friends, and even your staff will notice the difference and will thank you for it.

I will start with below the line, and I am sure you can all relate to this stage:

People who are below the line generally lie in BED.

B stands for Blame: We don't mean to do it or want to do it, but we simply do. We always want to point the finger, but remember when we point the finger, there are always three of our own fingers pointing back at us. Typically, when things are not going smoothly, when happiness is low, relationships are tough and frustration is high, we will tend to stay in this space.

E is for Excuses: We all do this every single day of our lives. We procrastinate, we come up with reasons why we didn't succeed, why we didn't have a go, and why we didn't try just one more time.

D is for denial: Denial is the trickiest one to truly understand or identify, because you don't know when you are in denial. It takes someone who respects you and cares about you to say: "Hey, this is what is happening in your life because you are not aware of it". It takes a third person to transfer it. If you drink a lot of alcohol, the fact of the matter is you are probably an alcoholic, but for you, it's just a few six packs each night after work.

It's going to take someone who cares about you to say:

"Hey, it's time to slow it down a bit", and for you to listen to what they are telling you. Otherwise, something is going to happen to your liver, you're going to be in trouble, and it might be too late. So don't get to that place. Any time you Blame someone, make Excuses or are in Denial about a situation, you are what we call a victim.

Nevertheless, the line of life is full of choices: you have the choice to spend your time below the line, or you can stand up. You can break the barriers down and truly embrace living.

The word above the line is OAR: Grab the oar and steer your ship in the direction you want to take it and get the results in life you want. You can have the love from your family you want, and you can have the relationship with your children that you want. If you want certain things in your life, which we all do, this is the place you need to spend the bulk of your time.

Still, sometimes you feel as though you are on a paddle boat, with one oar and you are paddling so hard to get ahead in life, but really, you are just going around and around in circles. So rather than working smarter and getting some support or even using a tool like this one, you work harder, until eventually, you are completely and utterly exhausted. So, you can no longer give of your time and energy, you spiral out of control, and you live your life as a Victim. What you need to do is understand what OAR means.

O stands for Ownership: Own your ship, whatever happens is about you, your choices, your actions, your behaviours, etc.

A stands for Accountability: Have some accountability for each decision, action and outcome that is delivered.

R stands for Responsibility: You have the ability to respond. The people who live above the line are called Navigators.

These are the people you see on TV, in sport, in arts, and in business. I think we all want to live above the line and we want to earn the right each day to live in this space. This is where you all need to be. It is important to understand that we all go below the line; everyone one of us, every day, but it's not about how often you go below the line. It is about how long you stay there. When I was 26, I nearly gave up again. Due to health challenges that were mounting again, I just stayed in BED mode. It took all of my power away and all of my confidence. Still, I then made choices in my life and took ownership and responsibility for my wife, my Mum, my family and for myself. I wanted a brighter future, I wanted to bring inspiration and hope to the world, and I wanted to help make changes in individuals each and every day.

How would you address your challenges in both your professional and personal world differently if you were to be above the line? How would you utilise the resources this world has at our finger tips more effectively? How would you interact with your family, friends and clients? How would you use the objections and excuses from the people around you differently?

For all of us to keep bouncing over obstacles, we need strength and determination, but we also need tools, because we all have bad days, moments and situations in our life that can drag us below the line into the victim space. I had my Mother, my family and my inner belief that I am on this earth for a great purpose.

Yet, it's amazing that some people make life seem effortless and simple. They achieve amazing goals with seemingly no struggle, breeze through the hardest days without breaking a sweat, and they seem to feel happy, even in the toughest of circumstances. These people are not different from you. In fact, they face the same feelings and anxieties. However, what separates the successful and the unsuccessful isn't genetic material or ability, but their mindset. They choose to stay above the line, they choose to be positive, and they choose to grab their OAR and steer their life in the direction that they want to take it!

We all know that life is in our hands and we control the outcomes of every adversity, every challenge and even every victory. A wise man once said: **"Do not allow success to go to your head nor failure to affect your heart"**. We will always learn far more from a loss than we will ever gain from a win. We can choose to see obstacles in front of us as a mountain too steep and not worth climbing, or we can see it as another great challenge. Brick walls are not there to keep us out; they are there to show us how bad we really want it!

Let's look into the mindset of a **Victim** and a **Navigator** in more depth.

No doubt, everyone knows someone who thinks their life is just too hard; they constantly complain and freely share with you regularly how unfair their life is. It is always someone else's fault why they are failing, unhappy and even depressed. It may be a friend, a work colleague, a family member, or it may even be you. It's important in life that we are honest with ourselves, that we can put our hand on our heart and be truthful to who we are, where we are and what we wish to become.

Some people feed off being a **Victim** and love the sympathy that is given when they are in a dark place; they don't want to change and they don't feel that they deserve to live a better life. When you are in this space, you are stuck in **BED**: you know when you are in this place, as you just want to pull the covers up over your head and to shut out the entire world.

Some phrases you might hear as a **Victim**:

- I can't do that.
- Life is just not fair.
- I wish life would just give me a break!
- Why me?
- My life is so unfair!
- I'm stuck counting my problems.

This creates a mindset shift and your entire world feels darker, duller and destructive. So, your mind sees things like:

- The glass always being half empty
- A difficulty in every opportunity
- Just not enough hours in a day
- It can't get much worse

Some real life and simple examples of a **Victim's** mentality that we all experience each day include:

- That would be right, trust me to get the red light!
- Far out, you've got to be kidding, its only 11am. Why is this day dragging out?

- I'm in the 8 items or less aisle and that painful person in front has at least 10 items. Who does she think she is?
- It's not my fault I'm late to work. How was I supposed to know that traffic would be bad?
- You just cut me off; did you not see my two tonne, four- wheeled, bright red car heading into your lane?!

When we are below the line, we forget that life is supposed to be enjoyable, and that every day is truly a gift that needs to be embraced and treasured. But, as we all know, life is all about choices and those choices can reshape, re-mould and redefine our future.

Let me give you an example of when I recently became a victim. I just finished a large speech in Melbourne at a National Nurses Conference with over 400 in attendance. A speaker's rating is 0-5, with a score of 5 being outstanding and rarely achieved across the professional speakers world. I received a 4.87 and my agent called and informed me it was the highest score he had seen and with over 300 completed surveys and comments this was something I should be very proud of. So I decided to read all the comments, I was really enjoying the comments however out of the 300, 299 were fantastic and one comment just sucked me in and consumed by thoughts. The comment read "Too Americanised, and far too evangelistic for my liking." I couldn't help myself but all I could do was focus on the one bad comment as opposed to the 299 good ones.

It's time we stop playing the **Victim** card, begin to live in the **Navigator** space, grab our **OAR**, take **Ownership, Accountability** and **Responsibility,** so we can take our life to new heights. You know when you are in this state of mind as you want to spring out of bed, you're excited about each day and are really engaged with life.

Some phrases you will hear when being a **Navigator:**

- Could be worse...
- I am facing a few challenges, but nothing I can't handle.
- I am loving life and all that it throws at me.
- I'm so lucky every day.
- I enjoy counting my blessings.

These phrases, in turn, shift the mindset, and now your entire world feels brighter, clearer and happier. Your mind sees things like:

- The glass always being half full
- An opportunity in every difficulty
- You laugh to forget
- Life could be so much worse
- I dipped below the line tody, but I identified I was a **Victim** and bounced back

Some real life and simple examples of a **Navigator's** mentality that we all experience each day include:

- Its only 11am, so there's much more time to get things done.
- Wow, I hope that the person who cut me off is OK; clearly, they are in a rush.
- It's not my adversity I'm facing, but rather, how I deal with it, so I'll be fine.
- Who can I help today to make their life better?

As mentioned earlier, a very important and powerful point with this principle is: **"It's not about how often you become a Victim that determines the health of your mindset, but rather, how long you stay there".** You can become a **Victim**, 50, 70, 100 times a day.

However, as long as you identify yourself as dipping below the line and spring board back above the line, the quality of your life, your mind and your future will improve out of sight.

This principle will, no doubt, assist greatly if you maintain accountability and work to be in control of your mind. However, the below ten habits have enriched and empowered some of the biggest stars on the planet; their simplicity might surprise you, and they are not just habits, but tools that you can embrace along your journey.

I believe these ten points can be the key to your transformation, along with mastering your mindset and living above the line.

1. **Set yourself unique and inspiring goals every single day**

    Jerry Seinfeld is one of the world's most celebrated comedians. He's also one of the richest. Since the final episode of Seinfeld aired in 1998, he's earned $3.1 billion in repeat fees. Seinfeld's success didn't come out of thin air. Instead, he used a remarkably simple productivity system to come up with the best jokes and funniest stories: Every day, he would write something. It could be a single joke, a funny anecdote, or even a full episode's script. After he'd finished writing, he would mark the day on a wall calendar with a red X. After a few days, a chain of crosses started to emerge on the calendar. Seinfeld's only goal was to keep the chain going every day. Whether it was a Monday or a Sunday, he sat down to write, and marked each day with a big red X.

2. **Before you sleep, summarize your biggest achievements**

    There's more to productivity and success than just setting goals. After all, it's easy to set goals and then ignore them. Before you go to sleep, look back over your daily to-do list and cross off tasks you've completed. Add any incomplete tasks to the next day's schedule and force yourself to complete them.

3. Wake up at the exact same time every day

Everyone knows the importance of going to sleep at the same time every night. Few people, however, know how important it is to wake up at the same time every day. Set yourself a 'wake-up time' and make sure you're alert, awake, and out of bed at the right time each morning. Whether you go to sleep at 10:00pm or 4:00am, make sure you stick to your schedule. Waking up at the same time every day helps to set your circadian rhythm—an internal body clock that keeps your body energetic, healthy, and focused.

4. Don't fall for multitasking

You've probably heard how important multitasking is for getting things done. Here's a little secret: it's really not that great. Multitasking sounds like an excellent strategy for getting work done. After all, what could be better than doing two tasks in the time it normally takes to do one? Its only problem is that it doesn't work far more often than it does work. The world's most successful people all have one thing in common: they focus on one goal at a time. From Steve Jobs to William Shakespeare, the world's best CEOs and artists always achieve one goal before starting on the next.

5. Don't spend too much time online

Most people waste a huge percentage of their work day online. Even if you're focused and attentive at work, you doubtlessly spend at least an hour or two browsing Twitter and Facebook once you get home. It's amazing what you can achieve when you dedicate time normally spent on social media to achieving your goals and transforming your life. Log off early and go for a run, develop your artwork, spend special time with your family, or expand your dream business!

6. Practice mindful eating for health and relaxation

Mindful eating is a Buddhist practice that asks you to do something simple: eat your food slowly and appreciate every single bite. It sounds silly, but it's an amazing way to do two things: eat a better diet and truly appreciate the taste of the food that you eat. Next time you're about to stuff down dinner, stop and appreciate the taste, the smell, and the texture of your meal.

7. Every week, reconnect with a friend or acquaintance

In France and Italy, workers take two-hour lunch breaks to socialise and reconnect with their friends and co-workers. In Hong Kong, businesses refuse to answer their phones from

12:00pm until 2:00pm due to the importance of taking time off for lunch. Does your rushed, fast-paced lifestyle make it difficult to sit down with friends and acquaintances for lunch? Set yourself a goal of catching up with friends every week for an extended lunch or dinner; your mind and body will appreciate it.

8. Write down your thoughts before you go to bed for a great night's sleep

Do you spend hours tossing and turning before you fall asleep? There are hundreds of reasons for insomnia to occur, but one of the most common is anxiety over your thoughts. Purge your mind of demanding thoughts by keeping a special diary on your bedside table. Whenever you find yourself worrying about something, write it down to deal with tomorrow. Not only will this help you fall asleep faster, you'll also wake up feeling refreshed, prepared, and ready to conquer last night's thoughts and ideas.

9. **Eliminate negative people out of your life**

Some people are emotional vampires. These people feed on your happiness and seem to drag you down below the line whenever you're feeling happy with your life. Lifelong Victims can be emotional vampires and a huge drag on your happiness, your focus, and your ambition. Write them out of your life to feel more focused and ambitious, as well as far more in control and happy.

10. **Avoid technology an hour before you go to sleep**

Technology is addictive, and using it too much (or for too long) can lead to tech burnout. Free yourself from tech addiction by turning off your computer, tablet, phone or TV at least an hour before you go to sleep. Not only will this give you some personal time to reflect on your day or read a new book, it will also help you to fall asleep quicker. Some researchers believe that using tablets before sleeping stops your body from producing melatonin, which is an important sleep hormone.

I think that it's important to attempt to look at just three habits that resonate with you right now as the ones that you need to implement and master first; we should never try to master all ten at once.

Otherwise, you will become overwhelmed and not change anything. I try to remember something that I learnt from Dr John DeMartini: **"When you invest in you, the world will invest in you. When you begin to love you, then the world will begin to love you, and finally, when you value you for the person you are and the difference you can make, the entire world will begin to value you".**

CHAPTER THIRTEEN
WHERE TO FROM HERE?

"Holding onto anger is like drinking poison and expecting the other person to die." Buddha

"The longer we dwell on our past misfortunes, the greater it controls the excitement of our future." Michael Crossland

Each day, there is a continual challenge for being truly in control of my health and my mental state. People ask me all the time how my health is, and my response is always the same: "Mentally, I'm in a great space".

I think that as long as we are mentally strong, then the days we are fortunate enough to spend on this earth will be days that we can truly enjoy, because our minds are in the right place.

I think I have and always will be so passionate and driven around the power of giving and finally I got a chance to give something to someone who has sacrificed so much in her life for me. The day that I put a pink ribbon on the door of a new home for my mum to live the rest of her life in was one of the greatest days of my life. I will never forget the tears in her eyes and the smile that she had in her heart. She was glowing with pride and joy. The feeling of happiness is so much greater when you give in this world as apposed to when you receive.

I recently found a lump in my throat. I underwent test after test, I was poked, prodded, X-rayed and scanned. During that time, I couldn't help but allow my mind to wander. I remember one morning I dreamed about what the doctors might say, and I got into the shower to try to clear my mind, because I had almost convinced myself that the doctors were going to tell me that, unfortunately the lump was a terminal cancer. I immediately vomited in the shower and I felt like I was going to pass out. I think in that instant I really began to understand the power of my mind. I realised that if I did not control it and have it in the best possible place, that my life could be a real mess.

The support that I have from my family, friends and social media followers is, at times, extremely overwhelming, and I certainly feel very blessed to have these wonderful people in my life.

I've begun to realise in my life that it is the people who are around the challenge who actually hurt more than the person who is actually dealing with it. I've begun to understand by watching my Mum deal with her emotional challenges that the people surrounding the people who worry the most actually hurt more, because these are the people who truly have no control, and I think that when you are out of control, you find it very difficult to deal with that situation.

Throughout all those years when Mum would receive my test results, her response to me was always the same: "Son, everything is going to be OK". But she knew deep down inside that was not the case. She carried that burden and the pain, so I didn't need to. It's amazing the sacrifices that some people in this world make to support other people. I think that is why I love that song, People Helping People, so much, because I regularly think to myself: Can you imagine if every single day every single one of us got out of bed and had a dream and a goal to simply just help people? I truly believe that it would be heaven on earth.

The results of that lump have finally arrived, and thank God for all his amazing work! It is benign. It will eventually require surgery, but there is a significant risk with the surgery, as it is tangled around my vocal chords, which could render it very difficult to speak if something went wrong throughout the surgery.

We are currently in the process of investigating a few heart issues. I'm not getting enough blood throughout my body, which is causing me to be very dizzy on a regular basis. I tried to ignore it for as long as I could, staying positive and thinking that it will just go away. I was recently speaking to the Essendon AFL team, and I became very dizzy on stage. I don't think that anybody noticed, but I thought I needed to "man up" and get some tests done.

Sometimes I try to deal with things by ignoring them, but whether the problem is personal or professional, this is not the way to go about it. A small issue swept under the rug can eventually turn into a massive trip hazzard. I will soon be going into hospital for a few days to try to work out exactly what is going on.

But in saying that, I'm in a great mental space, I'm so happy with my life, I dearly love my wife, and I have surrounded myself with wonderful people who continue to see me stretch and grow to become the best me that I possibly can be. This year alone, I have been on 126 flights around the globe and spoken to over 270,000 people worldwide.

I am an Ambassador for many different organisations and charities, including Camp Quality, Cancer Council, Australian Cancer Research Foundation, Limes Disease, and Hope for Haiti, and I have been the Australia Day Ambassador for the past six years.

However, despite being able to achieve little milestones here and there, I continue to get told what I can't do in life, and I love showing them that I can. Life is truly a gift, and I will treasure that gift until my last breath on this earth is taken. I simply just want to inspire people so that one day, someone might simply say: "Because of you, I didn't give up."

Thank you for being a part of my journey. I hope that you can reflect on my journey, and that it helps to inspire you to become the best you that you can possibly be, whilst paying good deeds forward towards making the world a better place.

Michael.

With smiles and passion in creating inspiration daily.

CHAPTER FOURTEEN

CONNECTING WITH MICHAEL

There are a number of ways you can connect with me on social media and the web, which include:

Website: www.michaelcrossland.com

Facebook: facebook.com/MichaelCrosslandcom-112483922154060

Twitter: twitter.com/mikecrossland

LinkedIn: au.linkedin.com/in/michaelcrossland

Instagram: www.instagram.com/michaelcrossland

Videos: michaelcrossland.com/videos

Amazon Author Page: amazon.com/author/MichaelCrossland

Hard copies of my book are available from Amazon or my website.

CPSIA information can be obtained
at www.ICGtesting.com
Printed in the USA
FSHW020021180119